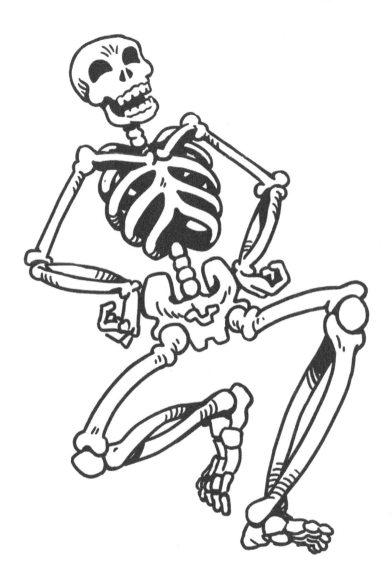

VIBRANTLY MORTAL

Why Engaging Death Enriches Life

Jeff Vankooten

To my hospice patients. You've taught me how to vibrantly live…

"Life should not be a journey to the grave with the intention of arriving safely in a pretty and well-preserved body, but rather to skid in broadside in a cloud of smoke, thoroughly used up, totally worn out, and loudly proclaiming "Wow! What a Ride!"

Hunter S. Thompson

"Even though we don't like to think about it, death is going to come no matter what, so we should learn to stare it down. Remember that death well handled is one of the surest signs of a life well lived."
Thanissaro Bhikku

"Analysis of death is not for the sake of becoming fearful but to appreciate this precious lifetime."
Dalai Lama

"Death is not waiting for us at the end of a long road. Death is always with us, in the marrow of every passing moment. She is the secret teacher hiding in plain sight, helping us to discover what matters most."
Frank Ostaseski

"To know and to feel that one goes around only once, and that the deadline is not out of sight, is for many people the necessary spur to the pursuit of something worthwhile."
Leon Kass

"I have cancer. And I know that once you get that diagnosis, no matter how much you already know, something happens, everything becomes much more real.
Ironically, it brings greater permission to be fully alive. I find it very exciting."

Ondrea Levine

FORETHOUGHT

I knew without a shadow of a doubt, in no uncertain terms, I did not want to go down there. The patient I had taken care of had passed three weeks previous and was being held on ice in the basement until the ideal time for the funeral. She was going to be cremated, so there was no embalming.

I knew that decomposition had set in, and that the body would have a pallid, waxy look. I also suspected that the decaying process had lent a putridness to the atmosphere. I did not want to smell that.

The body was in the basement of an old and well-worn mortuary. The floorboards creaked when you walked on them and tattered corners of carpet were being untethered from their origin. The lighting was dim and poor. Windows in this particular mortuary were mostly nonexistent.

The son of the deceased had gone downstairs in the basement to have his final farewells with his mom. I ministered to this family. On one level it was a noble and profound situation. The son gave up his job to spend his days as the primary caregiver for his dying mom. They lived in a trailer home and he kept it as close to normal for her as possible.

On another level it was creepy and bizarre. There was a very dependent relationship the son had with his mom. She definitely ruled the roost even near death. It reminded me of the movie "Psycho", Alfred Hitchcock's psychological thriller of a pathological relationship between mother and son.

That dynamic of noble care and creepy dependence defined my time with this family. I walked them through this process toward death for about 3 months.

When his mom died, at 94, I was summoned to the trailer home and provided solace the best I could.

When I arrived, the body was tenderly wrapped in the bed sheets and looked peaceful. Good care.
However, he wanted me to take a picture of him holding his mom's decrepit and darkened hands for posterities sake. Weird dependence, but not unheard of. I knew that this man was going to have a difficult time letting go of his mother.
The day of the funeral came. There I was, on the main floor of the mortuary, determined to not go down to

the basement. That was soon thwarted by the request of the funeral director, who asked me to go and see what was going on. The son had been down with his mom's corpse for quite some time.

I reluctantly worked my way down to the basement. The steps creaked as I went down and I rounded a corner past an old and noisy boiler. Again, this was an old mortuary, so the mortar on the basement walls was stained and crumbling. Low lighting and unswept cobwebs contributed itself nicely to the creepy atmosphere.

When I reached the bottom, I saw that the son had nicely dressed his mom on the gurney. She was indeed pallid and beginning to smell. He was also clipping the toenails of the corpse and kissing it numerous times on the cheek and forehead. A bit of a jarring sight and one that confirmed the unhealthy reluctance of a son to let go of his mother.

After I made my way to the basement, I encouraged the son to say his farewells and come upstairs for the simple memorial in the dank chapel attached to the mortuary. He did so, slowly letting go of her hand. After the simple memorial, the son, the funeral director, and I went back downstairs. It was the mother's desire that she be cremated. There was an old furnace in the basement that was used for the cremating. It was a bit greasy on the outside and was proof of the many fires that were stoked in it to consume an entire corpse.

The corpse was in a makeshift cardboard coffin. The son had done a good job making her look nice in her favorite clothes. The director and I wheeled the gurney, holding the body to the entrance of the furnace. The director pumped the gurney to a height that matched the front doorway of the furnace.

All of us there used our strength to push the body into the belly of the beast. I had never done anything like this before, nor had such a front row seat to a cremation. The door to the furnace entrance was closed and locked tight.

The son wanted me to push the button that actuated the fire. He asked me to wait as he counted down the precise time to do that. He wanted the time of this action to be precise and one he would remember in perpetuity. Like a conductor, he pointed to me to coordinate and push the button to fire up the machine.

The furnace rumbled at first and had a sound of compression that flared like a jet engine.
The small peep hole on the door allowed a close-up witness to the destruction and chaos inside.

I knew the son had not eaten in few days and offered to buy him lunch at a restaurant across the street. He was ravenous as he devoured the Italian dish he ordered. When he felt satiated, he was ready to leave. Since I had picked him up where he lived, to bring him to the funeral home and memorial, he got in my car and we began the journey back home.

Before that trip commenced, however, he wanted me to slowly drive down the alley next to the mortuary so he could see the smoke from his incinerated mom's body waft from the chimney into the atmosphere. I obliged and stopped for a time so he (and I) could engage in a ritual of remembrance...

PREFACE

There is a sociological and evolutionary theory called Terror Management (TMT). It was originally proposed by Jeff Greenberg, Sheldon Solomon, and Tom Pyszczynski and arranged in their book *The Worm at the Core: On the Role of Death in Life.*

The gist of the theory is that everything we do, from creating community and religion to balancing our checkbook comes in response to the fearful knowledge that someday we are going to die. That is, every human action and decision in life is taken (subconsciously or not) to ignore and avoid the inevitability of our own demise.

> *"To live fully is to live with an awareness of the rumble of terror that underlies everything."*
> **Ernst Becker**

Another theory called Meaning Making Theory (MMT) strives to anchor death in a more positive way, using it to create a better life and meaning. It states that we are meaning-making people and want to live a life that counts.

In fact, some of the preeminent psychologists

throughout history have tried to answer the question of what motivates us as human beings.

A man who survived the concentration camp in World War II is Victor Frankl. He became a prominent psychologist and developed a theory called "LogoTherapy." Its basic premise is that humans are meaning-making creatures and have the ability to find meaning in all circumstances, even despondent ones.

It also states that we have attitudinal freedom to choose how we will respond to life's challenges and circumstances, even death. This, according to Frankl, is the ultimate freedom. He stated that we do what we do because at our core, we are seeking meaning in our lives. That is, meaning is the central, core component of a life well lived. We do have the agency to respond to death in healthy and meaningful ways.

So, TMT intimates that fear of death drives what we do. MMT on the other hand, approaches the reality of death from a more positive stance, stating that a positive engagement with our mortality will enhance the overall meaning of our lives. I'm deeply committed to the fact that death is not the bitter end of a life. I'm firmly ensconced in the MMT approach to death. It's positive, and it's meaningful. Death is a part of our story and is a powerful teacher for a life that truly matters.

Engaging death has greatly enriched my life. As a hospice chaplain, daily trafficking in death and dying has changed who I am. It has altered my worldview and my life in powerful ways. Though fearful, the fear of dying has provided an impetus for a wonderful life. It compels me to engage with life in ways that are life-affirming. Really.

However, for most people in the developed western world, death is optional, just not a part of their narrative at all. It won't happen to me. It's not when, we think, but if. We don't want to think about it or engage it.

Death has never been more repressed than it is today in contemporary Western culture. The exclusion of death from the cultural conversation may be the preeminent characteristic of our age. To me this is unhealthy and detrimental to a life well-lived. For when we battle against death it not only minimizes its importance in our lives but contributes to its denial and the diminishment of our lives.

I want to change the conversation on death and the taboos that surround it. I'm going to take a different approach and make this less an informational, physiological book on death (a great book for that is: *The Thing About Life Is That One Day You'll Be Dead* by David Shields) and more of a motivational and inspiring one, using the reality of death as a springboard to a more fulfilled, enriched, and worthwhile life. It might easily fit under the self-help section in the bookstore.

Why choose death as a topic for discussion generally and an impetus for a meaningful life specifically? Am I a masochist? Demented? Abnormal? I have worked with death and dying on a consistent, daily basis, as a hospice chaplain. What I have learned and experienced with that has provided the fodder for living an urgent, important and sacrificial life.

Think about it. The topic of death is the most relevant to us as human beings and indeed the entire world. Death is at work in nature and wildlife. I asked a 93-year-old hospice patient if he was afraid to die. With a flippant clearing of his throat, he said,

"No. I mean how hard can it be, everyone's done it so far!!"

May his tribe increase!

"The art of dying graciously is nowhere advertised, in spite of the fact that its market potential is great."
Milton Mayer

Everyone dies. Everyone. The thrust of this book is that engaging our mortality can greatly inspire and enrich our life. In fact, I believe that is what we have to do and one of the only engagements that is going to give life any luster or substance. Death, besides being very relevant, can be the most inspirational, motivational subject on the planet. That is my premise for this book.

Engaging death in healthy ways increases our joy and vibrancy for life. They are two ends of a spectrum; life and death. When interacting with your mortality, you don't take the little things in life that bug you so seriously. You realize food delivered late at dinner in a restaurant is not the biggest hassle of the day. In fact, you might even have compassion for the waiter who is just as mortal as you and trying to navigate life as best he can.

We often say that those who work in hospice, near death and the dying, "get it." Life is more important than the petty issues with which we burn up most of our days. Every moment is precious.

"If I take death into my life, acknowledge it, and face it squarely, I will free myself from the anxiety of death and the pettiness of life and only then will I be free to become myself."
Martin Heidegger

I hope as you read this book that you'll see that engaging death will truly, deeply, profoundly, and wildly inspire and enrich your life in previously unbeknownst ways.

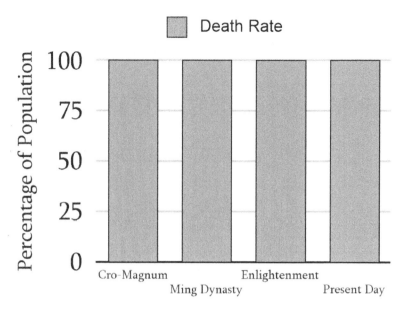

DEATH RATES THROUGH HUMAN HISTORY

INTRODUCTION

There was a treasure ship full of gold and precious jewels on its way back to port. About halfway there, it was approached by a pirate ship, skull and crossbones flag waving in the breeze, cannon turrets at the ready.

"Captain, captain, what do we do?" asked the first mate.

"First mate," said the captain, "go to my cabin, open my war chest, and bring me my red shirt."

Wearing his bright red shirt, the captain exhorted his crew to fight. So inspiring was he, in fact, that the pirate ship was repelled without casualties.

A few days later, the ship was again approached, this time by three pirate ships!

"Captain, captain, what should we do?"

"First mate, go into my war chest and bring me my red shirt!"

The crew, emboldened by their fearless captain, fought heroically, and managed to defeat all boarding parties, though they took some casualties.

That night, the survivors had a great celebration. The first mate asked the captain the secret of his bright red shirt.

"It's simple. If I am wounded, the blood does not show, and the crew continues
to fight without fear."

A week passed, and they were nearing their home port, when suddenly the lookout cried that ten ships of the enemy's armada were approaching!

"Captain, captain, we're in terrible trouble, what do we do?"

The first mate looked expectantly at the miracle worker.

"First mate, go into my war chest and bring me my brown pants!"

Our life is spent wearing brown pants. We are mortal after all. That reality literally scares the shit out of us. Death IS always under the surface of our lives rearing its uncomfortable, unpredictable, and terrifying head into our consciousness. We can smell it everywhere.

24

There is the inevitable confrontation with it. Our awareness of this human condition never ceases.

In fact, it could be said that our current diet culture and obsession with what we eat is a way to stave off our mortality. Mortality, however, continues unabated. Our brain's superior frontal gyrus sees to this pursuit neurologically, and our wrinkles see to it that our mortality goes unabated.

There was a time when death wasn't such a fearful event in North America. It was part and parcel to life. In an earlier time in North America if you grew up on the farm, you were around death all the time. Your favorite dog might pass, or your favorite pig was brought to slaughter. You may even have cut off the heads of chickens.

Since the immediate family all lived under one roof, it wasn't uncommon for mom to give birth in the kitchen and grandma to pass away upstairs; the circle of life. Houses were even designed to accommodate death. The idea of a parlor was conceived around death. Bodies were kept in the front room (parlor) of the house for mourning before taking it for the funeral. A parlor was often called a "Death Room" because of its use as a holding place for a loved one's body. Family, friends and relatives could visit a home's parlor and pay respect to the person who had passed. Fellowship, food, mourning and laughing all took place in the confines of a private home.

After World War II, with the improving conditions of life and a decrease in the number of deaths, the Ladies Home Journal suggested that this room was no more a death room. With so much "lively" activity now taking place in the home, the death room was now called "the living room." As a subtle result, death moved out of the house. Death became an event that happened outside the home and had no place in our rooms or our lives. The normalcy of death in everyday life began to erode and over time death became something to be greatly feared.

Death in popular culture began to take on terrifying undertones. Its portrayal in movies and books is not that of a welcoming, warm and fuzzy entity. In fact, the stereotype of death is someone in a black, tattered robe, holding a sharp scythe to reap a human life. A recent book I just read called *Death: A Life* by George Pendle was creatively written as death's memoir. Death explains his origin story as the product of Satan and his wife, Sin. Together they gave rise to death as we know it. Scary.

> *"I tremble to say there's good in death, because I've looked in the eyes of the grieving mother and I've seen the heartbreak of the stricken widow, but I've also seen something more in death, something good. Death's hands aren't all bony and cold."*
> **Caleb Wilde**

Why is death so doggone scary? It's not. The moment of death, in its simplest rendering, is the cessation of physical life with a sigh. All that separates this world from the next is a sigh. It's not scary. I've been there at those moments. Many of them. Though complications can occur up to that moment, the moment itself is not bad. It's simple. One small breath and it's over. It's like falling asleep. The wonder of hospice is the ability and expertise to make that moment as peaceful and meaningful as possible.

> *"It is the unknown we fear when we look upon death and darkness, nothing more."*
> **J.K. Rowling, *Harry Potter and the Half-Blood Prince***

"Your end, which is endless, is as a snowflake dissolving in the pure air."
Buddhist saying

"How fine is the mesh of death. You can almost see through it."
Jane Hirshfield

It's not death itself that scares us, it is the *thought and process* of death and dying that does. We just don't know for certain how it is going to be, how and when it is going come. Questions arise in our mind like: Will it hurt? Will I suffer? What will happen to me? Will I continue to exist in some way, shape, or form? What will become of the loved ones I leave behind? Have I left a legacy? Stressful stuff!

A moderate amount of fear regarding death is perfectly normal and part and parcel to what makes us human. In fact, that anxiety can be a powerful impetus to live a more vibrant life, from beginning to end. It can be a good thing.

However, fear of death can tip into the unhealthy, obsessive side of our psyche (thanatophobia). It can cripple us emotionally and suppress our joy of life completely. Nothing seems worthwhile, because, what the hell, we are all going to die anyway. Right? It can be debilitating rather than redemptive. There are some great psychiatrists and psychologists trained to help people navigate such deep-seated fear so life can be worthy to live again. Seek them out if needed.

"Some refuse the loan of life to avoid the debt of death"
Otto Rank

This book, hopefully, will help you move beyond the fear of your death in order to engage your mortality head on, to change your relationship to it, and live a more vibrant, abundant, and wild life as a result- to be *vibrantly mortal*. The chapters that follow are some surprising reasons death so poignantly enriches life. And that is what death is on some level, poignant...and certainly a part of us.

CHAPTER ONE: DEATH PRIORITIZES WHAT'S IMPORTANT

"If you are constantly aware of your mortal nature, you will only do what truly matters to you."
Sadhguru

"The price of anything is the amount of life you exchange for it."
Henry David Thoreau

Our culture lies to us all the time. The kicker is, we love the lies. We love to believe that the right product will make us worthy, or a material object will complete who we are as human beings. We hope that the right brand or social media connections will connect us to others and make us less lonely. The reality is that it's just not going to happen.

Our culture does not provide meaning. Oh, it believes it can, and we believe it does, so we continue to search for it in the midst of consumer culture. Maybe I can buy my way to a life that makes sense and provides a deep sense of significance and security. However, our culture is just not capable of that, no matter how compellingly it tells us it is. Yet we keep spending and searching…

So, our priorities and commitments can often be out of whack. We sacrifice true contentment at the feet of consumption.

If you knew your house was going to be destroyed by a wildfire, what would you take with you? You would start by making sure your loved ones were taken care of. Rescuing your pet(s) if you have any, would be another top priority. It is relationships we want to save and continue.

Most people when asked to evacuate their house, bring pictures that remind them of those important to them and a few trinkets that spur their memories for those they love. Rarely is it a computer, big screen television, etc. that is brought along. (I feel sorry for those people.) It is our relationships we want to prioritize in such an event.

Facing death head on jars us to consider what is most important in life. Things of the world seem to fade in comparison. What do I want to continue after I am gone? To whom do I wish to leave my legacy?
Have I immersed myself, and invested fully in a life-

well lived? Have I had the right priorities?

Maybe you have gone to a racetrack for a greyhound dog race. No matter what track you go to, the mechanical rabbit they use to lure the dogs into racing is named "Rusty." Rusty is nothing more than a fake tool made up to look like a real rabbit. It is nothing but a ruse. It is attached to the inside railing on the track and designed to follow that track on a pace faster than the dogs. Let the race commence!

The promise of "Here comes Rusty" is announced over the facilities loudspeakers. Excitement builds not only in the stands, but in the pens where the greyhounds are caged. They tense their muscles and breath heavily through their muzzled mouths with the anticipation of the "hunt." They each know that the faster they run, the better the chance of catching the prey.

Rusty, that inanimate and mechanical being, is released to the track. The whirr of the contraption can be heard throughout the track. At just the right moment, the pens of the dogs open, and they frantically clamor to get a foot hold on the dirt track.

Every once in a while, though, a greyhound will

actually catch the mechanical "rabbit." Guess what? That dog will never race again. It's discovered it's been duped, led to believe that what it was chasing was real. It's not. It's just fake, a fabrication. We can be the same. We pursue things in the hopes it will be real and provide satisfaction. Alas, no. We live in a day and age of perpetual desires constantly unfulfilled. We can squander so much time...

I uniquely calculated how much time we truly have to live on planet earth. I figured the average life span for most North Americans is 80 years (28,835 days or 692,040 hours). The human race (home sapiens) has been roaming around and doing what they do for over 200,000 years. So, I imagined what an 80-year- old length of life would look like from the perspective of 200,000 years. What is the reality of that relative comparison?

"Life is too short to be lived badly"
Marjane Satrapi

Well I found that in comparison to 200,000 years of human existence, an 80-year-old life bouncing in front of that time frame amounts to 13 seconds in relative terms. That is, 80 years looks like a mere 13 seconds from the vantage point of 200,000 years. In all of human existence, our normal life span of 80 years is whittled down to 13 seconds. If each second corresponds to 6 years, how do we spend the 13 seconds given to us? I calculated that too. So, here are our most common activities we do fill up that time:

Sleeping: 24 years. Sounds amazing but true. We spend an inordinate amount of our time on earth sleeping and dreaming. In fact, we also spend approximately 7 years trying to get to sleep! Using our relative metaphor of 13 seconds with each second equaling 6 years, we just used up 5 seconds. That leaves 8 seconds left in which to live.

Working: 13 years on average. That sounds short, and it probably is, but I calculated 8 hours a day for 5 days a week starting at age 15 and finishing up at age 65. Put all those hours together and it equals 13 years. My guess is with the frenetic work ethic in the United States it would be much longer.
Wouldn't it be great if we could get that all out of the way at once? Work 13 years straight and be done. Anyway, if we use our 13 seconds, factoring in longer hours for many, that's approximately 2 seconds of our lives spent working and grinding out a living.

That leaves us with 6 seconds left.

Waiting: Studies have shown that we spend 7 years waiting. Whether that's in a line, traffic jams, picking up children from school, downloads etc. we spend a lot of our lives just waiting. If we subtract another second (6 years) of our lives waiting,..

That leaves us with 5 seconds.

So, we haven't even gotten that far yet. From sleeping, working, and waiting, we are well over halfway done with our short life.

Entertainment/Screen Time: Entertainment is our way to escape the harsh realities of life. Maybe that's why we spend so much time immersed in it. It is a way to suspend what's hard in life and allows us to escape it. Today much of our entertainment is spent in the company of screens, whether that be our cell phone, large screen televisions or our computer.
Swipe. Click. Binge. Repeat.

Think now about how much time you spend on entertainment and screen time. When I calculated this a few years ago, we spent 18 years consuming it. Everything we do on the screen has proliferated in crazy accelerated ways. I think it is even more time-consuming today. But, for now, it's 18 years and is comparable to 3 seconds in our illustration.

That leaves us with 3 seconds.

Sleeping, working, waiting, entertaining takes up the bulk of our time.

However, I also found out that we spend 7 years of our lives in the bathroom, primping and defecating our way through life. So…

That leaves us with 2 seconds left- 12 years.

Those 12 years are also spent in various and sundry activities. We spend on average 4 years eating and drinking. It has to happen in order to survive. Calculating that in our relative, metaphorical example, leaves a bit more than 1 second of our lives intact. That second is also full as well. Prostate exams, trips to Mickey D's, making love etc..
What's left over is a minuscule amount to spend on things that truly matter to us in life. So…

Spend your life in pursuits in which love is truly exemplary.

Death compels us to do just that, prioritizing what is important, and helping us realize how fleeting life really is and how vapid it so often can be. Every second counts.

I've never heard anybody say its taken a long time to grow old…

"Existence cannot be postponed."
Irvin D. Yalom

"It is not that we have a short time to live, but that we waste a lot of it. Life is long enough, and a sufficiently generous amount has been given to us for the highest achievements if it were all well invested. But when it is wasted in heedless luxury and spent on no good activity, we are forced at last by death's final constraint to realize that it has passed away before we knew it was passing. So it is: we are not given a short life but we make it short, and we are not ill-supplied but wasteful of it… Life is long if you know how to use it."
Seneca

"Nobody works out the value of time: men use it lavishly as if it cost nothing... We have to be more careful in preserving what will cease at an unknown point."
Seneca

"We run after values that, at death, become zero...that's what dying patients teach you."
Elizabeth Kubler Ross

CHAPTER TWO: DEATH SHATTERS PRETENSE

I was fortunate in high school to play on a state champion basketball team. I worked so hard in practice and took shot after shot to become a prolific scorer. It was an exciting time for me. I loved my teammates and we learned the value of camaraderie.

Having the whole school get a day off to celebrate the championship was only the beginning. Our coach had shirts made with "State Champion" proudly displayed on the front. We got a trophy. We each got to take home part of the net we cut down after the game. We thought our shit didn't smell.
We were hot stuff!

Maybe the most important reward I got was the picture of my team who had bonded so closely over the game of basketball. We were in this celebration together and it was inspiring and comforting to see us all side by side, with our coach front and center. It was the same photo that made it into our yearbook to live in infamy. However, I went further than the yearbook. We had the opportunity to purchase a larger picture;

one suitable for hanging on the wall. I bought one. This was a big part of who I was.

Coming home from college I would look at that picture from time to time and reminisce. Sometimes the players that became such good friends would get together when we were home from our academic pursuits and talk b-ball and the incredible experience of winning state. I took good care of that large picture and stored it away where I hoped it would be safe. It made me feel important and special.

When I graduated from college and moved home for a bit to get my feet underneath me, I wanted to revisit the photo. When I found it in its normal resting spot, I noticed that my mom had folded the picture in half! In fact, the crease made its way straight down the middle of my likeness.

When I confronted my mom on her destructive deed, she was pretty nonchalant about it. She simply needed room in the closet and the size of the picture was hard to store, so she folded it so it would fit in an envelope that could be placed in a box.

It dawned on me pretty plainly and powerfully:

Life trashes your trophies

We can so easily think we're all that. We live with the cult of productivity and believe that what we are pursuing so strenuously is going to last. We all are involved in the rat race, yet we have never met anyone who has won it. Even if we did meet them they would still be a rat. We can live under delusions of grandeur and inflated self-esteem. The feeling we get from trophies, and indeed the trophies themselves, we find out the hard way, are indeed only fleeting. Trophies are external accomplishments, expressions, and approval of others that define us. That is the key word here; external.

> *"Our experiences, accomplishments, and approval are not ways to inform our identity, but ways to express our identity."*
> **Steve Tonkin**

Death brings about an honest assessment of who we are and our place in the universe. A properly balanced self-esteem is essential to a meaningful life. In other words, it's crucial to live out of an authentic identity with no pretense; inward, rather than outward.
If you define your authentic identity by what you do,

or what others want you to be, or what accomplishment they think is most important, you open yourself up to all kinds of disappointment- a trashed trophy. You are living in pretense, inauthentically and miserably.

An inauthentic life produces insecurity and feelings of insignificance. These lead to two classic behavioral traits: You will either find yourself *self- promoting* your ideas or needs to be recognized by others, or you will find yourself *self-protecting* by withdrawing and avoiding engagement with others.

It's the fear of being found out for being an imposter. Most people live on the edge of this insecurity their entire lives.

Letting our trophies (accomplishments, expressions, others) define who we are, rather than letting the core of our being define who we are is to only be pretending.

> *"You rarely have time for everything you want in this life, so you need to make choices. And hopefully your choices can come from a deep sense of who you are."*
> **Fred Rogers**

Authentic identity reflects the real you without the need to present yourself to others in a manner which conceals who you really are. Consider this: How much personal power are you giving away to others because you are overly subjecting yourself to their opinions of me, or comparing yourself to them?

Remember, that the process of discovering your authentic identity may take some time to grasp within the context of your life. Honestly reflecting on our mortality can accelerate that process. Better to know who you really are sooner rather than later.

The following is from a workbook my friend Steve Tonkin (stevetonkin.com) who developed a dynamic formula for discovering your authentic identity. There are three core questions, he states, that will help us live fully from who we are so that what people see of us, is what they get. An authentic self.

1. Why do I matter?

2. What intrinsically motivates me?

3. What are my personal values?

The answers to these questions lead to the real you. It's

a movement to define ourselves from inside out rather than from outside in.

Engaging death in an honest and realistic manner is essential for answering the first core question:

Why do I matter?

It's gets us to the nitty gritty.

> *"There must be more to life than having everything."*
> **Maurice Sendak**

It can best be answered by asking two sub questions.

A. What gives you a sense of significance or impact?

B. What gives you a sense of security or safety?

For some, the answer to these questions is money and material wealth. The one who has the most toys wins. I suspect this is the primary reason for significance and safety most people in North American find in life. However, making money is not a truly worthwhile impetus. Plus, who are you when it's gone or diminished? Material goods always play into the law of entropy- things degrade and decline over time. For others, prestige or reputation defines why they matter. They have to get to a certain level of accomplishment and recognition before they feel that life has meaning and that they have worth.

Many people answer the question by seeking a religious or spiritual insight. Why do I matter? God created me so I'm important. I am one with the universe. Worth is found in the transcendent.

Again, Victor Frankl, the father of "logotherapy" stated that a big component of finding meaning is contained in the Noetic dimension of life, that which is transcendent. So many situations and circumstances in life can lead to meaninglessness otherwise.

I think of the concentration camps Frankl endured. To survive in those camps, people found hope and meaning beyond themselves, the noetic, attaching them to some higher power or purpose.

"Noetic refers to states of insight into depths of truth unplumbed by the discursive intellect. They are illuminations, revelations, full of significance and importance, all inarticulate though they remain; and as

*a rule, they carry with them a curious sense of
authority..."*
William James, philosopher

You need to think long and hard for the answer to the question, "Why do I matter?" Everything flows from there.

*"There must be a lot more to life than being really,
really, really, really, ridiculously good looking."*
Derek Zoolander

The second core question to discover and live out of your authentic self is:

What intrinsically motivates me?

That is, what truly gets you out of bed in the morning? What honestly motivates who you really are deep down inside? The word intrinsic is an adjective that means belonging naturally; essential. It is the set of qualities that expresses who you are naturally, with no pretense, your natural propensity.

Understanding intrinsic motivation will not only help you to know what drives you, but also what drains, demotivates, or often causes you relational difficulties.

48

More about discovering this can be found at www.stevetonkin.com/what-is-intrinsic-motivation.

The third core question gets down to your personal beliefs and plays a significant role in every action, communication, and decision that you make.

What are my personal values?

Or what matters most to you?

These core values are different from the first core question. The first core question explores your innate value as a human being regardless of any utilitarian value you give to society (Trophies).

Your core values are different from your interests. Interests are expressions of your core value and not definitive of who you truly are. Your core values are mostly informed by your parents, your training, and your life experiences. When these core values are consistent with our authentic self, we begin to express these values as our own.

Once you answer the three core questions, you can begin to recognize your expressions as authentic or inauthentic. Our expressions are what other people see us displaying and what they must interact with. You will have many ways that you express yourself.

Expression is required for a healthy identity but should not define you. (Inward truth rather than outward definition must do that.)

Engaging our mortality helps even the playing field, whittling down who we are to the very essence of authenticity. One of the regrets dying people have is that they didn't live true to themselves but let others dictate who they were.

Theologian Eugene Peterson said that many of us go through life impersonating ourselves. He was highlighting the natural tendency we have to wear masks, to put forth an image of ourselves that isn't truthful in order to manipulate how people respond to us.

We wear masks to hide personality flaws or insecurities. Heck, I read other people's blogs and hear other people speak and think I'm not anywhere close to their level. It is that insecurity that often has me grabbing for the mask of being more intelligent or humorous than I really am. It's exhausting to maintain an image.

A friend of mine, McNair Wilson, a former Disney Imagineer, and, as he puts it, a professional third grader, says in his creativity workshops that you must be you "actual size". That is, be no more or no less than what you truly are. So, how do you be your actual size? You must be vulnerable with two people.

-You must be brutally honest with yourself.
This entails confronting those aspects of yourself that make you brilliant as well as the dark sides that hinder you. You can't hold back or be afraid of what you might find when you let your guard down and confront the totality of who you are.

How do you know the totality of who you are? The answer: only in relationships with others. They are mirrors and conduits for feedback on who you truly are. Good friends should move beyond being nice with one another toward an honesty that cares deeply for the growth of the other. We all need friends who love the truth more than they love us.

What have others been revealing about yourself over

the years? What have those closest to you seen as your flaws? What drives them nuts? What wonderful things have been said about you over the span of your life? What qualities do they seek out in you? Is there a personality pattern that emerges?

-<u>You must be completely vulnerable with the other</u>
There is a contemplative, intentional community in France whose mission is to be "*fully vulnerable, and fully available*". Sounds noble and appealing but man, is that a hard thing to do! We are laden with defense mechanisms to protect ourselves from being fully vulnerable and full of excuses to avoid the inconvenience of being fully available.

To be completely vulnerable with others means you have an inner fortitude and a healthy enough ego that is able to share with others the most intimate characteristics of who you are; what you see is what you get. The ability to share your thoughts and emotions helps build security and safety into our relationships – and strengthen our esteem and ego in the process.

Now there is always the risk that people will take your vulnerability and abuse it or use it against you. Thus, you can't be vulnerable with everyone (be cautious on Facebook) so stick with the friends in your life who know you best. They'll use that vulnerability in ways that minister to your heart and your soul.

Try today to share one intimate reality of you who you are with a close friend or spouse and see what happens. I've found that nothing but good comes from it.

There was an unemployed man looking for work. He found an opening at a zoo that was looking for someone to dress in a gorilla costume and sit in a cage. The real gorilla, the star attraction, had passed away and they didn't want to let the visitors know.

He figured he could that. He applied, got the job, and began to sit in the cage in the gorilla costume. He got bored so he began to jump around and act "gorilla like". He found out that the more animated he became with the gorilla moves, the more elated the audience became. He was intoxicated with the accolades, so he thought he would really work the crowd.

He began swinging on a vine, and on his third pass he slipped and flew right into the lion's cage. He realized he was in grave danger, so he began to tell the audience that he really wasn't a gorilla, he was only dressing up in a costume and they needed to get help. Before he could get the message completely out, the lion pounced on the man, pinned him to the ground and said, "Would you shut up! Do you want to get us both found out?!"

Most people spend the first half of their lives being what others expect them to be. They then spend the second half of their lives being what they were made for in the first place. But why wait til' then to become an authentic person?

Becoming who you really are requires some bold moves.

-First you must get out of your costume. Undress yourself from market definitions of who you are supposed to be. Become unbranded from product lines and become your own brand. Do the hard work of discerning what expectations from others are accurate and which are unreasonable. I think your gut knows the difference. This will make you a new person.

-Then become free from your cage. If ignorance is bliss, then we have a lot of contented people in the world. Don't believe everything you read or hear. Ta the time to think and determine where you are being locked in by biases (yours and others), past disappointments and other restrictive components of life. Change and healing begins with you. Often our cages are locked from the inside.

-<u>Finally, venture out into the wild</u>. The philosopher David Henry Thoreau said that the "mass of men lead lives of quiet desperation." Often what is called resignation is in reality desperation. Out into the wild is really a part of the life you live now. To be out of your costumes and free from your cages opens a whole new adventure for the life, like the one you are already living. Doing this will give you a whole new purpose.

CHAPTER THREE: DEATH LEAVES A LEGACY

My maternal grandfather was one of my best friends. When I could, I would meet him and his buddies at a place called "Chuck's Donuts". It was a hole in the wall place, a greasy spoon for donuts. Though good, most of the delectables were just laxatives in disguise.

Anyway, those mornings became a precious and integral part of my week. There, we would laugh and cry, as he passed his wisdom down into the young mind and heart of his grandson. It was great. It was real.

I would also visit his house on many summer afternoons and do a little porch sitting. He always sat on a classic glider couch rocking with rhythm to the sounds of the crickets. I remember that he would have the news on the television in the living room for us to hear, and he would wield a fly swatter like a well-trained ninja.

There, our conversations would continue, and the relationship would further deepen. Sometimes, there were no words exchanged, but a silent camaraderie existed just the same.

When I got the news that someday I had long known that I would someday receive it was a shock none the less. My grandfather had fallen down the basement stairs and cracked open his head. It didn't sound good. He was not going to recover. So, I did what anyone would do when they get a call like that about a loved one. I dropped everything I was doing and quickly headed to the hospital to be by his side.

There I found him in a room, lying unconscious on a gurney, with his mouth full of blood. The overflow was trickling from his mouth and following the deep creases of his beautiful, aged face. There was nothing more they could do for him. I used towels that I found to gently wipe and clean up the overflow of blood as best I could. I found myself taking care of my best friend who was nearing the end. Surreal.
Yet, I was grateful to have this brief time alone with my grandfather.

When the rest of the family arrived to hold vigil over the patriarch, I noticed a change in his condition. The machines that weren't keeping him alive but only monitoring the strength of his existence on this planet indicated he was waning.

I went over to my grandfather, brushed the little tuft of hair on this head, and whispered invitingly, "Big guy, it's time to go home". No sooner did the resonance of the word "home" come out of my mouth, did he flatlined. At that precise moment.
Right then. My cousin on the other side of the bed knew the profundity of that moment. It didn't dawn on me until later the impact that moment would have on me.

You see, my grandfather held me in his arms when I came into the world, and I held him in mine when he left the world. We shared a complete and powerful generational circle of life.

Death is around to make room for the next generation to take our place. Life needs the wisdom of old age and the exuberance of youth, both together. In order to complete the circle and move humanity forward we need a replacement system. Death does just that. It's essential for the survival of our species.

The amazing thing, when I think about it, is how much of a legacy my grandfather left not only for me but also for my children. Though he passed away before they were born, a part of him is in them and my memories of him keep him alive in their thoughts and ancestral history.

The *Day of the Dead* (Spanish: Día de los Muertos) is a multi-day celebration originating in Mexico. In Mexican culture, death is a normal part of life and thus should be celebrated through the ancestors who have passed away.

Their belief is that they help and encourage the spirit of the deceased to continue moving on the other side of this life. Altars are built in honor of their loved ones and remembrances and celebrations are conducted there and at gravesites. I celebrate the *Day of the Dead* (November 1-3). I find it less morbid than Halloween.

Think about the people in your life who have shaped you. Your ancestors. Whether you met them or not, their spirit courses through your soul, helping define who you are. Build a shrine to them in your home somewhere for a time or visit their gravesite and reflect on their impact on you and future generations.

"The ones who love us never really leave us."
J.K. Rowling, *Harry Potter and the Prisoner of Azkaban*

"Death? Why this fuss about death? Use your imagination, try to visualize a world without death! . . .Death is the essential condition of life, not an evil."
Charlotte Perkins Gilman

"Existence is nothing other than a perpetual alternation of life and death, composition and decomposition. There is no life without death, there is no death without life."
Claude Bernard

CHAPTER FOUR: DEATH AMPLIFIES BEAUTY

"And day to day, life is a hard job, you get tired, you lose the pattern. You need distance, interval. The way to see how beautiful the earth is, is to see it from the moon. The way to see how beautiful life is, is from the vantage point of death."

Ursula K. Le Guin

In her seminal book, *A Pilgrim at Tinker Creek*, Annie Dillard deeply explores the wonder in the corner of the world at Tinker Creek, in the Blue Ridge Mountains. It is completely rooted in observations of the natural world, and it won the Pulitzer Prize for non-fiction in 1975. It's a beautiful book.

The unknown narrator is very self-aware and alert to every detail, going into exquisite descriptions of the wonders of the natural world, fully aware and fully present. Einstein said that "nature conceals her mystery by means of her essential grandeur..."

Our knowledge of mortality can expose the many everyday wonderlands hidden before our eyes. If we would just open them.

"Cherish the beauty of life not despite its perishability but precisely because of it; because the impermanence of things — of seasons and lifetimes and galaxies and loves
— is what confers preciousness and sweetness upon them."
Pico Iyer

It is bone jarring emotionally and faith shattering to bury a child. It is agonizing. The thought of the act still is many years later. I have presided over a few now and I never want to do one again. It's the ending of a story which has hardly begun.

I remember one particular gravesite service I presided over. It was a beautiful spring Colorado day, with not a cloud to disrupt the rich blue of the sky overhead. It was being held at a special place dedicated solely to the graves of babies and children. It was known as *Babyland*. A sad place, *Babyland* was situated on a higher bluff where you could see the entire front range of the beautiful Colorado Rockies. Dispersed throughout this parcel of land were some gravestones shaped liked cradles and hearts. Stuffed animals and toys were left by loved ones next to the markers to commemorate a life that had ended much too soon. There is a cruel juxtaposition of child-like innocence with adult ramifications.

The child I was burying was a two-month-old baby named Desiree. She was the first child of a young couple in their twenties. They were a bit rough around the edges, with the exuberance of youth tattooed on their arms and pierced in their noses and ears. They were wonderful, but you could tell they were shell shocked over their loss. Both looked through eyes which were empty, indicating that their current reality of the world offered nothing of worth to their lives.

The casket that held Desiree was a miniature one, all white, with stuffed animals attached to the top. It was a cruel reminder of the futility of life as it sat above an open hole ready to be lowered down into the confines of the earth, the innocence to be covered by the earth's detritus.

There were about a dozen helium balloons of various colors available, one for each participant at the gravesite that morning. It was a surreal scene: two young grieving parents, a deceased two-month-old little girl in a casket, and colorful helium balloons held by grieving family and friends.

The intent of the service was for me to officiate with prayer and some comforting words (if there can be any in that situation) and then hold a simple celebration of life for Desiree. Then each person would simply and silently release their helium balloon into the atmosphere.

I don't remember much about the memorial other than the grieving young parents and the helium balloons. When the celebration and remembrance of Desiree's short, precious life was concluded, the balloons were released.

Every one of them caught the same thermal draft and sailed en masse to the West on their way to the Rocky Mountains. It was beautiful. The shimmer of the sun off the inflatable objects made them look like precious gems floating against a backdrop of translucent blue. It was beautiful, in stark contrast to the gravity of the day.

As the draft carried the armada of balloons almost out of sight, you wondered if you could even see the balloons anymore, they were soaring so far away. Everyone shielded their eyes and squinted to get as close an examination of the sight before us as possible.

As I surveyed the atmosphere, I found one balloon that caught my eye. Barely perceptible. I had to really focus to see it. As I watched the last remnant of that balloon fade into oblivion, I noticed a bright star appear that took its place. As the balloon disappeared it seemed to morph into a star. A star was shining...

What was interesting to me was it was around noon in the springtime. Normally not a time for stars to shine. In fact it is so rare an occurrence, it is considered a phenomenon, in the general usage of that word, something extraordinary or outstanding.

It took a few moments to gather my senses and calibrate my seeing to the wonder of a star shining in the middle of a bright sunny day. When I realized what I was seeing, I summoned Desiree's young parents over to me. I pointed to the location of the star and guided them until they could locate it too; shining in the midst of the bright day. I reverently pointed out that that was Desiree. Desiree was giving us all a sign that all was okay, and the wonder of life never ceases to exist. That is, at the core of the universe is love.

An engagement with death, wakes us all up to the wonder and the beauty of the world all around us.

> *"Beauty is how objects end. Beauty is death."*
> **Timothy Morton**

> *"Death is the mother of beauty."*
> **Wallace Stevens**

Adam Gopnik, an American author and essayist, gave reverence to the bleakest season as a necessary counterpoint to the exuberance of spring, harmonizing the completeness of the world and helping us better appreciate its beauty — "Without winter", he argued, "we would be playing life with no flats or sharps, on a piano with no black keys."

Aesthetics is a branch of philosophy that concerns itself with the principle of beauty and artistic taste. The quintessential Japanese aesthetic is known as *wabi-sabi*, "Beauty of things imperfect, impermanent, and incomplete." When the Japanese break something like a vase, they repair the crack by filling it in with gold. They believe something is more beautiful when it is damaged and has imperfections.

Death allows us to be electrified by the beauty in the world and see with our damaged and mortal bodies how beautiful we and our broken world truly is.

"Life is a big fat gigantic stinking mess, that's the beauty of it, too."
Gayle Forman

"Life is beautifully tragic. Giving it up isn't the hard part; it's the living part that everyone struggles with."
Allison Blanchard

"This universe is the wreckage of the infinite on the shores of the finite."
Swami Vivekananda

"I don't think of all the misery but of all the beauty that remains."
Anne Frank

"Our life is a faint tracing on the surface of mystery."
Annie Dillard

I recently received a card from a dear friend and colleague of mine. I find myself reading and re-

reading the words that where inscribed in it:

"..the most visible creators I know of are those artists
who express the inexpressible- with out brush,
hammer, clay or guitar.
They neither paint or sculpt- their medium is being.
Whatever their presence touches has increased life.
The see and don't have to draw. They are the artists of
being alive..."

Being Vibrantly Mortal is to paint your life with beauty.

CHAPTER FIVE: DEATH INSPIRES A WHOLE ASSED APPROACH TO LIFE

"Without an ever-present sense of death life is insipid."
Muriel Spark

"There are few things in the world as dangerous as sleepwalkers."
Ralph Ellison

My wife and I both work in hospice. We make our decisions on whether it will harness the wonder and dynamic of life or whittle away what precious time we have on this rock. We get it. That's what that job will do to you. We don't waste our time. We know we only have 13 seconds. We do so much, between bluegrass concerts, travel, and drinking craft beer, that a friend of ours said we don't "half ass it", we "*whole ass it.*"

So, if, at a fork in the road, we wonder if we should go home or take a 45-minute detour to a brewery we haven't been to before, we ask ourselves what a whole ass decision would be. Even if a concert is happening on Wednesday evening at 9, in the dark cauldron of winter, we will decide whether to go or not based on the Whole Assin' philosophy and outlook on life. We usually go, weather be damned.

This isn't to be confused with freneticism and pursuing total exhaustion and burnout. Nor is it about throwing all caution to the wind and not giving a fuck. All the activities we partake in enrich our souls on some deep level. Sometimes Whole Assin' It is partaking in rest and relaxation, Whole Assin' It R&R style.

This concept is hard to articulate (you either get it or you don't), but the following is a short list of tenets to a Whole Assin' It philosophy on life. It adheres to the principle that "quality" of life trumps "quantity" of life. Follow some of these or adopt the attitude and stance of this philosophy toward life and you will become a part of the elite Whole Assers club!

Whole Assin' It instills adventure

Adventure doesn't necessarily have to mean an African Safari or jumping out of an airplane (though it could mean that for some). Whole Assin' It asks one to view life as an adventure no matter how mundane. If you have an awareness of your ultimate demise, you will make decisions in life predicated upon the fact that all of life (marriage, kids, taxes, dinners, friends, etc) is all part of an adventure if we allow it to be. It matters and deserve our attention and exploration in the here and now.

My wife and I have certain responsibilities now that we are fully engaged in and see our present state as an adventure. Not long from now though, Lord willing, our Whole Assin' Lifestyle dream is to buy a Mercedes Sprinter van, deck it out so its livable, and hit breweries around the country recounting our adventure with a blog called "Hops and Highways." Truth be told, the breweries are simply an excuse to provide a road map to explore this great country of ours.

We also see all of life as an adventure. We don't necessarily have to leave our front door to experience adventure. Sitting in the sun on our back patio is enough to get the contentment juices flowing and be excited.

Most of my patients in advanced age say they are bored and lonely. They reflect fondly upon the adventures they had in life and wish they could partake in them once more. In fact, it is in the recall of their adventures that they find solace in their present boredom. These adventures live on in their hearts and their minds. Reflecting upon death now, embarking on adventures no matter how small or mundane they seem, can be a great preventer of intolerable boredom not only now but then.

"To die will be an awfully big adventure."
JM Barrie, *Peter Pan*

"The big question is whether you are going to be able to say a hearty yes to your adventure."
Joseph Campbell

"You needn't die happy when your time comes, but you must die satisfied, for you have lived your life from the beginning to the end . . ."
Stephen King, *The Dark Tower*

Whole Assin' It embraces the fragility of life

The thing about life is that it ends. Physical life anyway. There is a Greek parable popularized by the Roman philosopher Cicero in 45 B.C.E. about a tyrannical King, Dionysus, who had a courtier named

Damocles who was more than willing to flatter the King. Once Damocles mentioned to the King how wonderful and opulent the life of royalty must be.

The King decided to let the courtier sit upon his throne and experience the life of royalty to find out for himself how great it is. He provided Damocles with the finest of foods, the most pristine service by beautiful wait staff, and the finest of perfumes.

The courtier was feeling incredibly spoiled and he liked the life of a royalty. However, after a time, Damocles noticed the King had dangled a razor- sharp sword over his head attached only by a thin, single horsehair. Realizing this fact, the courtier pleaded to go back to his simple lot in life. Damocles realized how tenuous a life of wealth, power, and prestige really is. Knowledge of a looming death gave him the impetus to live a simpler life without all the hassles, knowing that death comes to all regardless of their lot in life and life is, after all, hanging by a thread.

I had a patient who was in his mid-sixties, a strapping, handsome, athletic man. The reason he was on hospice was he had a diagnosis of "Mad Cow Disease." It is a transmittable, progressive, and fatal disease affecting the central nervous system of adult cattle.

A human version of mad cow disease called variant Creutzfeldt-Jakob disease (vCJD) is believed to be transferred to humans by eating meat contaminated by the disease. It affects about one person in every one million per year worldwide; in the United States there are about 350 cases per year.

What was unique about this case, however, is that the doctors weren't sure meat was the culprit and were baffled by how this otherwise healthy man could contract Creutzfeldt-Jacob disease. This man, and his illness, was in my spiritual care.

His diminishment was swift. This was a man who had been a ski instructor 6 months earlier, who now, was in a skilled nursing facility on hospice.

Under hospice care, we periodically have care conferences with family to introduce the hospice team and go over any questions or concerns regarding the patient's care. This particular care conference was tinged with great sadness. Here was a young man, vibrant just months ago, without any recognition of who we were. This once strong man was now relegated to a hospital bed.

As we sat around the table with the family, the man's spouse stated that this "was not what we planned." Damocles' sword. That statement haunted me deeply and embedded itself for ever in my approach to life. You just don't know what the future holds. You can be in the prime of life and have something unexpected, beyond your control, invade your life in a moment.

As I write this, a friend of mine's 25-year-old marine biologist son was recently run over by a boat while snorkeling. The propeller severed his arm completely and threatened the loss of his legs. It is inspiring and agonizing, both, to read the mom's posts as she balances on the fine edge of despair and hope, tinged with a deep confusion of why him, why now, and what next.

Life is fragile. Very fragile. As you age, you become more and more fragile. In light of this, my wife and I are determined to engage in our adventures sooner rather than later. Would you rather hike the Rocky Mountains when your knees are still good and you know you are healthy, or wait for some unknown time when nothing is certain or guaranteed?

Another couple I ministered to also solidified my

Whole Assin' approach to life. The husband got dementia in his early seventies and was placed on hospice. Not that it always plays itself out, but you are eligible for hospice if your qualifying diagnosis, as it progresses "normally" and will limit life to six months or less.

As I visited this dying man in the memory care unit of the nursing home, I spoke mostly to his wife. She pointed out to me, with eyes moist with grief, that their lifelong friends are now enjoying their retirement with cruises and world travel. "Here we are," she said, "spending our days in a memory care unit. Not what we expected at all."

The health club where I work out is in the basement of a medical office building. It was originally intended by the hospital to be a place of therapy for patients as well as a benefit to employees. It's quite nice. I leave feeling invigorated from the exercise.

Yet, every time I leave, I can't help but feel a bit sanguine. You see, on my way out to the parking lot I have to make my way through the elderly and infirmed who are there to see their doctors. Many times, there are vans with lifts helping down patients in wheelchairs. Walkers are ubiquitous as the aging joints no longer seem as spry or lubricated as they once were, and extra help is needed to walk and move forward.

I'm glad I encounter it all though. It keeps my life in perspective and gives me a renewed vigor for the present moment. Soon, much sooner than I would like, I will be in their shoes. My joints will be worse off than they are now (though mine do ache from time to time). I'm sure there will be many visits to the doctor just to keep the effects of old age under control. I already have a couple "liver spots" on my hand for goodness sake.

I also participated in a funeral service today for a dear friend who passed away at age 50 (50!) from melanoma. Talk about an event that keeps things in perspective and compels one to make the most of every moment.

All that is to say, we should wisely reallocate resources from the future (whether it be money or time) and use it for the service of the present. There are friends to see, places to go, and family to love. Time moves quickly and we never know how soon our life may end. What, then, is all that disproportionate worry about future comfort and security etc. going to do for us?

I'm not trying to be a downer here, but I believe the healthiest thing we can do is look in the mirror and admit to ourselves that we are aging and are going to die someday. It's a powerful habit to engage our mortality. It's scathingly honest and eliminates all kinds of dysfunction and psychosis. It keeps us on our toes. It also helps us live today no matter what our age.

Maybe the most wonderful gift we can give ourselves and others today, is quite simply, today. Live it now, live it fully, and live it well – because for heaven sakes time is swift and unpredictable. I'm not much of a philosopher (makes my head bust open), but I am passionate about life, and life becomes more meaningful when I filter it through the prism of dying.

"What do we have to hold on to? Only the certainty that nothing will go according to design; our hopes are newly built wooden houses, sturdy until someone drops a cigarette or match."
Pico Iyer

"If we're not reflecting on the impermanent nature of life, then there are a lot of unimportant things that seem important."
Allison Choying Zangmo

Whole Assin' It makes decisions in the here and now

Life is the process of aging and aging is the process of death in all of us. That is the primary plot line of our lives. Living into, and acknowledging that reality, is the most powerful thing you can do to live a fulfilled and meaningful life. Therefore, it is critical that you engage the finitude of your life. There is no better impetus for us to live fully than our own death and mortality- to be vibrantly mortal.

Patients near the end of their lives overwhelmingly express the hope that their lives were meaningful. Social scientists have discovered 4 conditions for finding meaning in life:

-To be valued by others

-To have a purpose to live

-To experience a life that is integrated and whole

-To connect to something grander and greater than ourselves.

One needs to be intentional about creating a meaningful life day by day in light of one's finite nature. Every moment counts. It prompts us to remember, reflect, and respond in light of that fact, so it becomes a powerful impetus for us to pursue the priority of the important rather than the *tyranny of the urgent.*

The tyranny of the urgent usually consists of those tasks in our day that intrude upon us for immediate attention and are easy to accomplish. These are mostly managed with time. They're also not that important. Answering emails, checking texts, meetings, etc. are all urgent but not critical to a meaningful life. We can easily hide in these tasks the majority of our lives and avoid the difficulty and vulnerability of the priority of the important.

The priority of the important consists of those tasks that are essential to leading a meaningful life but are hard to do, managed not by time but by attention. What are you mostly paying attention to: the urgent or the important?

The important tasks usually involve attending to the vagaries of family and friends, engaging in a crucial conversation, the maintenance of a marriage, etc. Daily exercise or meditation are also hard to do but important to a healthy, meaningful life.

Every day, every moment, ask yourself to remember, reflect, and respond on your life, and prioritize your attention, not necessarily your time, so that the tyranny of the urgent doesn't squander the priority of the important. Managing your attention this way will help remind you what is essential each moment in pursuing a life of meaning, purpose, wholeness, and transcendence.

"It is the ever-present danger of losing life which helps to bring home to us the value of life."
Karl Popper

Despite our wondrous technologies and scientific advances, we are nurturing a culture of diffusion, fragmentation, and detachment. The thesis of a very important book by Maggie Jackson entitled *Distracted* posits that the way we live is eroding our capacity for deep, sustained, perceptive attention – the building block of intimacy, wisdom and cultural progress.

She writes that:

"Increasingly we are shaped by distraction…the seduction of alternative virtual universes, the addictive allure of multitasking people and things, our near religious allegiance to a constant state of motion: these are markers of a land of distraction…This is why we are less and less able to see, hear and comprehend what's relevant and permanent, why so many of us feel that we can barely keep our heads above water, and our days are marked by perpetual loose ends."

Time marches on and there isn't anything we can do about it; except change our attitude and perception toward it. One of my favorite scenes is the monologue by the character Mitch, played by Billy Crystal, to his son's fifth grade career day in the movie *City Slickers*. Up to this point he has been pondering the unrelenting advancement of time and his meaningful(?) place in it. His attitude and perception are not only humorous, but very evident:

"Value this time in your life kids, because this is the time in your life when you still have your choices, and it goes by so quickly. When you're a teenager you think you can do anything, and you do. Your twenties are a blur. Your thirties, you raise your family, you make a little money and you think to yourself, "what happened to my twenties?" Your forties, you grow a little pot belly you grow another chin. The music starts to get too loud and one of your old girlfriends from high school becomes a grandmother. Your fifties you have a minor surgery. You'll call it a procedure, but it's a surgery. Your sixties you have a major surgery, the music is still loud but it doesn't matter because you can't hear it anyway.

Seventies, you and the wife retire to Fort Lauderdale, you start eating dinner at two, lunch around ten, breakfast the night before. And you spend most of your time wandering around malls looking for the ultimate in soft yogurt and muttering "how come the kids don't call?" By your eighties, you've had a major stroke, and you end up babbling to some Jamaican nurse who your wife can't stand but who you call Mama. Any questions?"

Imagine there is a bank that credits your account each morning with $86,400. It carries over no balance from day to day. Every evening it deletes whatever part of the balance you failed to use during the day. What would you do?

Draw out every cent, of course!!

Each of us has such a bank. Its name is TIME. Every morning, it credits you with 86,400 seconds. Every night it writes off, as lost, whatever of this you have failed to invest to good purpose. It carries over no balance. It allows no overdraft. Each day it opens a new account for you. Each night it burns the remains of the day. If you fail to use the day's deposits, the loss is yours.

There is no going back. There is no drawing against the "tomorrow." You must live in the present on today's deposits. Invest it so as to get from it the utmost in health, happiness and success!

The clock is running. Make the most of today.

To realize the value of ONE YEAR, ask a student who failed a grade.

To realize the value of ONE MONTH, ask a mother who gave birth to a premature baby.

To realize the value of ONE WEEK, ask the editor of a weekly newspaper.

To realize the value of ONE HOUR, ask the lovers who are waiting to meet.

To realize the value of ONE MINUTE, ask a person who missed the train.

To realize the value of ONE SECOND, ask a person who just avoided an accident.

To realize the value of ONE MILLISECOND, ask the person who won a medal in the Olympics.

Treasure every moment that you have! And treasure it more because you shared it with someone special, special enough to spend your time. And remember that time waits for no one.

The awareness of my mortality has encouraged me to no longer waste time. I realized my days have been subdivided into smaller and smaller units of efficient, urgent time. Not good.

I have lost reverie. Reverie is a state of being lost in one's thoughts; to daydream. When is the last time you daydreamed? When was the last time you deeply pondered a sunset, or sprawled on the grass with your arms behind your head letting your thoughts wander with the movement of the clouds? If, like me, it's been a while, then you are overly distracted.

We are in essence not nurturing our inner selves when we lose reverie. I encourage you to go ahead and waste some time every day. Don't let the efficiency bug infect you.

Give yourself permission to go against the speed, expectations, and distractions of your life. Don't respond to the annoying "ping" of arriving email – stay focused on the task at hand. Shut off the television and read a book for two hours straight (think you can?). Don't check Facebook or Twitter for a whole week. Have a three-hour dinner with good friends. Let go of the guilt for wasting time.

You'll be a more interesting and deeply peaceful person as a result.

"Listen to your life. See it for the fathomless mystery that it is. In the boredom and pain of it no less than in the excitement and gladness: touch, taste, smell your way to the holy and hidden heart of it because in the last analysis all moments are key moments, and life itself is grace."

Frederick Buechner

Whole Assin' It delights in the monotonous

The theologian G.K. Chesterton stated that more theology of life can be learned in a nursery than in any textbook written. He wrote an essay in his book *Orthodoxy* entitled *The Ethics of Elfland*. It is one of the most powerful essays I have ever read.

In it he praised the power of fairy tales. They are fantastical tales of imagination that convey truth through the medium of wonder and adventure. It is an adult medium as much as a child's.

The problem today is that we have lost most of the wonder that conveyed so much truth for us as children in fairy tales. In other words, we are no longer like children.

The basic gist of the essay is how magnificent the ability of fairy tales are for revealing deeper meaning for us as adults. He goes on in the essay to talk about the qualities of children that open up meaning for us as adults.

The difference between adults and children, he believed, is wonder. Think about a child. They ask you to throw them up in the air and catch them.
When you finish it once, they will ask you to "do it again." And then "again." And then "again." Children delight in the monotonous. It's wonderful.

Think about God. He tells the flowers every spring to bloom and then tells them every fall to go dormant. He then asks them to do it "again".
And then "again." And then "again." God delights in the monotonous.

We usually do everything we can to escape the monotonous through entertainment. We've lost the wonder in everyday events and tasks.
If God can delight in the monotonous and we can't, maybe we've outgrown God.

With our imaginations awakened, we can see with

new eyes our own world filled with wonder once again.

A new study revealed that average bodies are as appealing to others as men who have six pack abs. That is good news for the majority of us who either by genetics or by lifestyle have bodies that are, quite simply, average.

Due to time constraints and shifting demographics, less and less families are sitting down at home to share a common table together. They seem quaint, unrealistic and outdated these days. Average. They are mundane it's true, but how critical they are to communal health.

It seems to me that most of the ills we are experiencing today is because we didn't want to be average. The mundane was something to be avoided and seen as a roadblock in our pursuit of excellence.

The creation of exotic mortgage packages, our overspending, and intense sports activities for the kids are all symptoms of our flight from normalcy.

The point? All of our striving today and our frenetic attempts to be "excellent" may not be the best thing for us. We are conditioned by the myth of progress and the tug to be outstanding to believe that everyday life just doesn't cut it.

Yet it is everyday life with its dirty dishes, pesky weeds and average tasks that ground us in reality and provides the greatest joy.

Being average doesn't mean mediocrity. It does mean that every moment of every day is spent unleashing the power of average. How wonderful!

"Do not ask your children to strive for extraordinary lives.
Such striving may seem admirable, but it is the way of foolishness.
Help them instead to find the wonder and the marvel of an ordinary life.
Show them the joy of tasting tomatoes, apples and pears.
Show them how to cry when pets and people die.
Show them the infinite pleasure in the touch of a hand.
And make the ordinary come alive for them.
The extraordinary will take care of itself."

William Martin

Whole Assin' It has no regrets

Another way of saying this is to not "should" on yourself. And if you do, don't step in it. I remember in the late eighties and early nineties Apple computer was near bankruptcy. Steve Jobs had been ousted from the company he co-founded, and it was on the brink of extinction. Stock in Apple Computer then was around $15 a share.

I remember thinking that I should buy some shares. I believed in the product and just had a hunch they weren't going to disappear.

Currently Apple stock is soaring these days. Even buying a small amount of stock when I was thinking about it would have given me a windfall, I still would be reveling in. I SHOULD have bought Apple stock in the late 80's early 90's.

The problem with "should" is it causes guilt and regret.

A big part of a Whole Assin' It attitude is not to regret the past. It doesn't "should." Regrets so often can be an anchor that weighs us down and hampers a positive movement forward in life. There is no use hoping for a better past. It isn't going to happen.

"You can't go back and change the beginning, but you can start where you are and change the ending."
CS Lewis

"It is never too late to be what you might have been."
George Eliot

Whole Assin' It is communal in nature

You must be in a human, unmediated (beyond the screens and bits of technology) relationship with other people. There are two types of relationships in life: Social connections and intimate bonds. Social connections are mostly those people we know only superficially. There are those we connect with through social media and online. We know who they are and what they do mainly through their social profiles. Not much of substance is exchanged. You're just popular but not significant in their lives.

We live in a day and age of social media and online connections. We shouldn't be lonely, right? We really shouldn't go it alone. Yet loneliness is an epidemic among young people. I say that young people today are living under the weight of irony. "Isn't it ironic", they say to themselves, "that I have over 2,000 friends on Facebook but can't find someone to hang out with me on a Friday night?" Even if they do, the relationship is usually superficial.

It's one thing to have a social network, it's another thing completely to have intimate bonds. Intimate bonds connect you to those people who know you inside and out and are available to you at any time, for any reason. These are people who are truly vulnerable and truly available. That's hard to do.

That dynamic is reciprocal. Most people are blessed if they have one or possibly two intimate bonds in their life.

You become significant when a few people pour themselves into your life and you pour yourself into theirs. Of course, the better and more honest the people in your life, the better and more honest will be your assessment of yourself.

Only a few people will be intimate enough with you and for you that you can truly trust them and feel like you are not alone in the world. This is a blessing and a gift.

I live under the diagnosis of bipolar depression. Back in college I didn't know what I was suffering from, other than the bone jarring depression that would keep me in bed and rear its ugly head often in those days. It was, and still is, horrific.

My roommate and best friend was aware of my deep emotional pain. He was the only one I really shared my depression with. You know, confusion and stigma and all. Sometimes those signs could be subtle and being bipolar I could often put up a good front while agonizing inside.

Anyway, one afternoon he noticed the signs of my beginning to slip into depression. He knew. He knew I was beginning to spiral into darkness. That afternoon, I'll never forget it, he got me off the couch and prodded me to take a walk around the neighborhood where we lived. But it just wasn't any, ordinary walk that afternoon.

You see my roommate gave each of us a "Swisher Sweet" cigar. Do you remember those? They were thin cigarillos with a flavored tip. I liken them to the "Boones Farm" (remember that?) of cigars. Anyway, we walked in silence (just being present can be all you need from somebody) and smoked our "Swisher Sweets."

It took probably 45 minutes to completely smoke the cigars. By the time we were finished, we returned to the house where we lived, and my mood was drastically lifted upward. I was going to make it for another day.

Here is the question when it comes to intimate bonds: Who are your "Swisher Sweets?" Who is the person in your life that can walk alongside in your pain and frustration? Who is the person that gets the vagaries of life and can empathize with you? Even another question comes to mind: who are you a "Swisher Sweet" for?

The Japanese are some of the longest living people on the planet. In addition to diet and genes, they attribute much of that longevity to the concept of Moai. These are social support groups of four to five people that are aggregated at childhood and continue on into the 100's. Such connection and support is healthy not only for the body, but for the soul. Swisher Sweets.

We can have similar Moai in our own lives. My

grandfather was a regular at a coffee shop for 35 years. Plenty of friends and support came from that time and place. I laugh that I am now my grandfather, a regular like him, at a coffee shop. I've been going for over 20 years now and some of my deepest male friendships have developed as a result.

I feel very blessed. My Swisher Sweets, my Moai, help me navigate my bipolar depression and encourage me to whole ass it every day.

Whole Assin' It takes health and wellness seriously

"People who contemplate the end actually behave in healthier ways- and therefore may actually live longer."
Eric Baker

Being mortal means our physical bodies decay over time. Even mental functioning can decline. But attending to the holistic side of who we are every day is essential to a life well-lived.

Whole Assin' It tinkers in curiosity.

Apollo 13 was launched April 11, 1970 and was the seventh crewed space mission of NASA's Apollo program. It was also intended to be the third meant to land on the moon. The mission was aborted due to internal, mechanical issues.

On the way to the moon, the Apollo 13 space craft encountered what the astronauts reported as a "pretty large bang." One of the fuel tanks exploded and ruptured, leaking gas into space. It decimated the main lifelines for the astronauts of power, oxygen, electricity and propulsion.

So, what became the main issue was not the blown tank, but the fact that as a result, the air filtration system was no longer working and needed to be fixed; fast! The astronauts of Apollo 13 were slowly suffocating to death.

The command center in Houston had to find a way to replace the filtration system with one that worked. The challenge, though for the NASA engineers, was they could only design something using material that the astronauts had available to them in the space craft.

Using tube socks, cardboard from logbooks and other

material available on the module, the engineers designed a system that successfully filtered the air and saved the astronauts.

What the engineers of NASA did was an example of bricolage. "Bricolage" is a French word meaning to tinker or putter about. It is the process whereby something is constructed or created from a diverse range of available things. That's the key to Bricolage: to use available things.

Using only the material on hand, that you have to work with, is the main limitation. In other words, it's making great use of very little things. We are limited in our bodies, our talents, our finances, our time, etc. but that doesn't mean we can't create and do great things we what we have.

Whole Assin' It tinkers in curiosity. It explores all available material and options and does with them the most extraordinary things.

It flows between two questions: "So what?" and "What if?", Those two questions are always being asked and answered in order. "So what?", tinkerers say, "if my arm was severed snorkeling," "What if" I get back to that activity I love so much? What would that look like and what do I need, given my current situation, to make that happen?

Ask any physicist and he'll tell you there is a whole lot of missing information when it comes to explaining the workings of the world. A blind spot. A gap in our information-gathering abilities.
Equations are always incomplete.

Physically, we all have a blind spot in the structure of the eye. There is a blind spot blocking out visual information where nerve connectors and receptors come together to form the optic nerve. We literally are not getting the full picture. To compensate our brain fills in the empty space of information to try to make sense of what it sees.

Experts swoop in to fill the empty space in our knowledge of the world and ourselves. Organizations pay them lots of money to provide the elusive information that will complete them and the lives of their employees. But even their insights are incomplete. They do not have the full picture nor the final answer.

None of us truly is an expert no matter the number of academic degrees. Maybe a curious instigator is who we need to listen to instead for explanations. Our own curiosity and being interested more than being interesting are key components to building relationships and conversations around issues that matter most to people. Get enough curious instigators together and you've got the makings for a real breakthrough.

Here are some qualities of curious instigators:

-They are found everywhere because everyone can be one.

-They are relentless in pursuing new avenues of knowledge and looking at situations from different angles.

-They worry less about being interesting and focus more on being interested in the conversation, person, or project at hand.

-They aren't afraid to push up against the status quo.

-They're playful in their approach to life.

-They are wildly open to the opinions and ideas of others.

-They never believe they have the final answer on anything

-They read what no one else is reading.

-They do something, anything, to get started.

Whole Assin' It yucks it up

"Laughter is by definition healthy."
Doris Lessing

"If we all couldn't laugh, we would all go insane."
Jimmy Buffett

.

At one point in my keynote presentation on "Resilience", I ask the audience to tickle each other. Within seconds, with no desire to do so, they laugh.

I stop them and ask them what was so funny? They agree it wasn't that what I asked them to do was humorous. It was actually uncomfortable. But, laughter can release tension. Someone said once, that laughter is the "heart sweating." It is a critical way to navigate the difficulties of life with vim and vigor and perspective.

Ask most comedians and they will tell you their best material comes from deep pain. The best jokes take something awful and make it silly. Psychologist Daniela S. Hugelshofer hinted that humor acts as a buffer against depression and hopelessness.

I read a very interesting book entitled, *Deep Survival: Who lives, Who dies, and Why*. In it the author, Laurence Gonzales, tries to determine the reason that some people are heartier than others in surviving disasters. He discovered that one of the deeper emotions survivors mine is humor. It is a release of tension and fears that dangerous situations produce.

The author discovered that laughter makes the feeling of being threatened manageable. It's about being cool. It's about laughing with an attitude of bold humility in the face of something terrifying.

The best humorists and comedians make us laugh at life because it is a deep way we can make sense and poke fun of the burdens of life. Survival humor is not the surface "ha ha's", but a deeper understanding of how the brain works in discovering and facing the reality of the situation.

Being a mortal that wants to be vibrant, when was the last time you laughed?

Life is hard. Life is confusing. Life is short. Reflecting on mortality and the brokenness of life through humor is one of the surest ways to get through it. Humor helps us process a complex world which helps make us who we are.

Since death is such a fearful subject, it's probably why those who work in hospice tell death jokes and are jovial about the vagaries of death. It's never to be disrespectful. Hanging out with hospice nurses can be a real hoot.

- What's Blonde and dead in a closet? The Hide and Seek Champion from 1995.

***

-A couple of New Jersey hunters are out in the woods when one of them falls to the ground. He doesn't seem to be breathing, his eyes are rolled back in his head.
The other guy whips out his cell phone and calls the emergency services. He gasps to the operator: "My friend is dead! What can I do?"

-The operator, in a calm soothing voice says: "Just take it easy. I can help. First, let's make sure he's dead." There is a silence, then a gunshot is heard. The guy's voice comes back on the line. He says: "OK, now what?"

***

-A man hasn't been feeling well, so he goes to his doctor for a complete checkup. Afterward, the doctor comes out with the results.

"I'm afraid I have some very bad news," the doctor says. "You're dying, and you don't have much time left."

"Oh, that's terrible!" says the man. "Give it to me straight, Doc. How long have I got?"

"Ten," the doctor says sadly. "Ten?" the man asks. "Ten what? Months? Weeks? What?!" "Nine..."

***

"If somebody has a bad heart, they can plug this jack in at night as they go to bed and it will monitor their heart throughout the night. And the next morning, when they wake up dead, there'll be a record."

Mark S. Fowler, FCC Chairman

CHAPTER SIX: DEATH AMALGAMATES SPACE AND TIME

I don't know why certain words come to me when they do. I doubt I even have heard the word "amalgamate" before, but then it revealed itself as I was thinking of this chapter. It means to combine or unite to form one organization or structure. That is, death brings together space time to form one coherent whole.

Einstein postulated with his theory of relativity that space is a substance and time is only relative, not absolute. That means there is leeway in the physics of the universe and how it works. Strange. For instance, he said the faster one went to the speed of light, the slower time would become. In fact, the source of gravity is the bending and dynamic of space and time interacting with each other. Time and space interface to be closely related. It's rather amazing.

However, we live such earthbound lives, often lacking the imagination to postulate what may be in existence before our very eyes. We live, after all, in an Einsteinian universe and not primarily in a Newtonian one. Yet, we persist in believing everything works according to a plan and that what you see is what you get. Like precise clockwork.

The new perception is that there is way more going on in the world than we can comprehend or explain. Time, too, flexes according to the physics of space.

I was called one afternoon to attend a death of a patient. The call was from her caregiver, who was a bit shaken on the phone. She asked if I could come as soon as possible.

The aged woman who had passed away, employed this caregiver for over two years to provide companionship and care to her. Inevitably, a deep and rich bond of love had sprung between them.

On this particular afternoon, the woman was sitting on the couch and motioned for her beloved caregiver to join her there. After some small talk, the woman leaned her head on the caregiver's shoulder and instantly died.

In the grand scheme of things that is a good and tender death, a peaceful way to go. What was miraculous about that moment was what happened at the cessation of that earthly life.

The caregiver shared with me that at the precise moment of death, the window in the room suddenly opened, and the digital clock by her bed began to flash the exact time of death. Almost like there was a power surge that disrupted the electrical flow and turned the clock suddenly back on.

When I arrived, the window was indeed open allowing a gentle breeze to enter. The clock by the bed was, indeed, flashing the exact time of death. It was compellingly eerie and profound at the same time. A commingling of space and time.

Whenever I attend a death, and minister to the family, I always tell them they are standing on sacred space. The profound atmosphere in the room is palpable. Regardless of what any of the people in the room may believe about life and death, everyone agrees that they are involved in something amazing; miraculous even. Something profound has just happened.

Every death I attend convinces me that there is more going on in life than we can hope to understand or explain. Space and time commingle to bring a more tangible reality to life that we can barely comprehend. Death brings us closer to that realization.

Once, I went to a hospice volunteer appreciation luncheon. There was a brief program and then a video was shown highlighting personal testimonies of volunteers walking alongside those who were dying.

One particular story in that video haunts me to this day. This particular volunteer recalled how he would visit a man weekly who was a professional magician in his younger days. Now in his eighties the man would fondly reminisce with the volunteer about the wonder of his life as a magician. He even shared a secret or two of the tricks he performed, especially the closeup magic.

The visits continued for about 8 months, and each time the elderly man would "talk shop" about magic and life.

One particular afternoon the volunteer received a call that the man he was volunteering for was asking for him. He went to see the man he learned to love so much.

When the volunteer walked into the room, he noticed the man was lying on his hospital bed pointing to the ceiling and introducing some of the biggest names in magic- Houdini, Harry Blackstone Sr., and others to the volunteer. He spoke to each one as if they were actually present in the room and could interact with his conversation.

This continued for a while, when the bed bound man asked the volunteer to sit by his side. He asked the young man to get close so he could say something to him. He continued to ask the volunteer to get closer and closer until he was eye to eye with the dying man. At that moment and distance, the man whispered to the volunteer that he was now going to show him the greatest magic trick he had ever performed. He was going to make himself disappear.

When assured the young man was ready to witness this great trick, he said some words to the ghostly magicians in the room, snapped his fingers, and instantly died. Poof. Gone. Magic.

As I've said, I have been present at the precise moment of death. It IS like magic. An amalgamation of space and time.

There is a concept in physics arising from Einstein's theory of relativity. According to the math, the existence of black holes is necessary to accommodate the bending of space and time. Recently, the first telescopic picture was taken of a black hole, proving their existence.

Everything we know about the universe could change if we knew for certain what happens to information inside a black hole. The reason we can't know that is the gravitational pull of a black hole is so immense that anything getting near it cannot escape its powerful pull. Even light cannot escape the gravity of a black hole.

Before that happens though, there is a moment before the information is lost known as the black hole's "event horizon." A black hole is bounded by a well-defined surface or edge known as the "event horizon" within which nothing can be seen, and nothing can escape, because the necessary escape velocity would equal or exceed the speed of light (a physical impossibility).

Every death has an event horizon, the boundary that

defines this world from the next, or this existence from something else. No one so far has been able to escape the event horizon of death, though there are many movements to attempt just that. I'll talk a bit about that in the chapter called "The Future of Death."

So, engaging your mortality makes you think differently about the physicality of your life and the way you use time. Confronting death will, hopefully, inspire us to see our bodies as sacred, and time as precious. Space and time act in concert at the event horizon of death, helping focus our attention on what matters most with our physical and spiritual being.

CHAPTER SEVEN: THE FUTURE OF DEATH

Human beings like to tackle issues confronting humanity. One being the elimination of death.

In the book, *Homo Deus*, by Yuval Noah Horan, the author states that the big issues confronting humans now and in the future are aging and death, the right to happiness, and being able to wield control over our biology and destiny. Humans want to pursue bliss, immortality, and divinity.

With the advent of science, death seems to be a slap in the face to our newfound, "godlike," powers. And if we can provide control over our biological systems, we will be as gods, living forever in complete happiness (with drugs and other technological manipulations providing that).

There is a philosophical movement known as "Transhumanism." Its basic tenet is that the body is simply a machine, and if the machine parts wear out or become damaged, they can be replaced with a technological counterpart. In other words, given the power of technology, we will be able to overcome our biological weaknesses and replace them with technology. This will make us then, into the higher image of our ideals (Homo Deus).

The technological and biological interface is already occurring. Knee and hip replacement, as well as other protheses are just a few examples of our technological prowess overcoming biological deficiencies.

Transhumanists believe that there will be a time when our technology will meld with our biological machinery to eliminate death, dust, and decay completely.

One is reminded of Mary Shelley's horror masterpiece, *Frankenstein.* Shelley was haunted by the specter of death, having experienced the death of her own baby as well as losing her own mother in childbirth. The technology of the industrial revolution provided fodder for her to contemplate the idea of immortality.

The excited talk in the salons and coffee shops of those days was of "galvanism". The Italian scientist Luigi Galvani discovered that an electrical current that ran through a severed frog's leg would result in a hopping and an animation of life in that limb. He moved on from experiments on simple life forms to deceased humans. He showed that electric current applied to the appendages of the dead could animate a body with moving hands and feet.

Prodded on by that technology, an 18-year-old Mary Shelley set out to write what became known as *Frankenstein; or, the Modern Prometheus*. It became a profound thesis on the scientific quest to control nature and thereby, our own biological limitations. It illustrated the god like abilities we might have to resurrect the dead.

Frankenstein's creature is still being pursued but without the negative connotation of what technology, melded with biological flesh, means. Transhumanists see it as our right and duty to use the technology we develop to further manipulate and advance the human species.

The focal point of science today is what British philosopher Stephen Cave calls the "Mortality Paradox"- If nature decrees for us physical degradation and death, then we must master that nature by our own devices and overcome its limitations.

Even now, the quest for immortality through technology is being pursued in mind-boggling ways.

There is the whole field of cryogenics where human bodies and heads (brains) are flash frozen as close to the time of death as possible and stored in frozen stasis in the hope that our technology will deliver the ability to reanimate that brain or body.

I think this is not much different from the ancient Egyptians preserving their deceased bodies to help them navigate the new or upcoming world they were to experience. Frozen corpses are the modern- day mummies.

There is a conviction among some transhumanists that there will be a time when we can upload our minds into the vessel of an artificial body and head, an abandonment of our biological bodies. That consciousness may even exist in some sort of "cloud" that is a continuation of who we are, limited only by iterations of more downloads.

I think of the movie *The Matrix* where the protagonist

Neo discovers our reality is literally simulated with computer code.

There is a classic episode of *The Twilight Zone* that explored just that reality some 50 years ago. It was called the "Trade Ins." The episode introduced us to an aged married couple who went to an organization that could transfer all of who they were individually into younger, more pristine bodies. Like a storefront window displaying its wares, the couple was guided past various models of youth that they could choose to transfer themselves into.

The issue with the aged couple, though, is they only had enough money to transform one of them. Since the man was in so much pain, together they decided it would be him that would undergo the procedure.

The procedure completed, the man was now a strapping, handsome, 20-year-old. He jumped around in exuberance declaring the lack of pain and the vitality of renewed energy. What had he become?

To ponder an answer to that question, in the thought experiment *Theseus's Ship*, Poseidon's son, Theseus, sails to Crete to kill the monster Minotaur. As a remembrance of that great battle, Theseus' ship is preserved in perpetuity. As the wood rots, over time, it is replaced with new wood over and over again. The question is: Is that still Theseus's ship or something else?

In other words, what does it mean to be human in this new technological day and age? Is what we create to solve the problem of death, dust, and decay really us, or something else? Same with upgrades. Is that still us or someone (something) else?

All that is to say that we are desperate to solve the problem of death. It is, after all, part and parcel to the core of who we are. The fear of death has driven homo sapiens to build magnificent structures, start complex religious systems, and to develop incredible civilizations. Yet we still have not solved the major problems of what it means to be alive. What does it mean to be human in this day and age?

"I don't want to live on in the hearts and minds of my countrymen. I want to live on in my apartment."
Woody Allen

Question: *If you could live forever, would you and why?*

Answer: *"I would not live forever, because we should not live forever, because if we were supposed to live forever, then we would live forever, but we cannot live forever, which is why I would not live forever,"*
Miss Alabama in the 1994 Miss USA contest.

CHAPTER EIGHT: WHAT I BELIEVE ABOUT DEATH

Only the three of us were in the room, and the husband lay dying. The only light was from a floor lamp in the corner of the room. It made for a somber atmosphere. His wife of over sixty years was gently caressing his arm, while keeping vigil over the love of her life. Now her husband lay in a hospital bed, next to the one they occupied together for so many years. Surreal. As I was present in this profound and tender moment, I was deeply struck by something she said. She interrupted her gaze, reserved primarily for her husband, and looked intently into my eyes. Hers were hazy from sorrow, a mixture of dread and confusion. Then she quietly stated to me:

"This isn't how the story is supposed to end."

Is this how the story of our lives is supposed to end? I mean, what is up with that anyway? That finality to life is depressing and not very hopeful. As a hospice chaplain, I've spent much time with the dying and have held the hand of someone at the moment of their last breath; the "end" of their story. Or is it?

Life is the process of aging, and aging is the process of death in each and every one of us.

That is the preeminent plot line of our lives. We are narrative-formed people after all, and each of our lives is a story with a motley crew of characters and plot lines that twist and turn as we age. For some that story is short. For some it is harsh. For some it is long. For some it is privileged. There are as many stories as there are people who have ever lived on planet earth, but make no mistake, all of them end in death.

Is this how the story is supposed to end? I thought about that in the context of writing a story. When wanting to complete a thought, an author ends a sentence with a period. If an author, however, wants to continue a thought, and only take a pause in its progression, he or she uses a semicolon. It is a reprieve in a continuous thought.

Death can be either a period, ending a story, or a semicolon continuing a narrative to be told beyond this mortal life. That semicolon for you might be a belief in the afterlife or the belief that your accomplishments and values will "linger" long after you are gone. There is a wonderful movement in the mental health realm called the "Semicolon Project." People who support the project get a semicolon tattoo. It is dedicated to confronting the tragedy of suicide head-on, with the byline, "Your story is not over." The choice of perspective is yours. We all yearn for immortality somehow; for life to persist. Death seems either to put the kibosh on that or provides an entry point to it.

"I intend to live forever—so far, so good"
Stephen Wright

I have to confess that I am a Christian and approach life from a Christian worldview. It answers for me the four core questions for understanding life more adequately than any other world view I've explored:

-Origin: Where did it all come from?

-Meaning: Who am I?

-Morality: What truly matters, really?

-Destiny: What happens at the end?

Without diving into each of those (there are other

great books dealing with that), let me outline for you the fourth worldview question: what I simply believe happens at the end:

This line represents the accumulation of a lifetime. We are naturally going along in a direction toward death, dust, and decay which cannot be stopped or postponed. It's not just a human predicament, but a condition affecting all life.

Somewhere along that line we confront another line, vertical to the lifeline. This is our death. For some the path to that line is long. For others it is short. For some it is happy. For others very sad. But we all must confront it on our lifeline. Again, I see this as a semicolon and not a period in a life narrative.

At that point we find ourselves face to face with the end of our earthly existence. Again, this is an event horizon. A boundary from which no one can escape and no one with certainty can know what happens after.

Yet, in my worldview there is a continuation of life beyond this earthly existence. For me to exist on the other side of death there must be a continuation of who I am. To believe that takes faith. Faith takes me over the threshold of death. I've learned to realize I am only a sojourner, a member of the human diaspora, that yearns for and knows there is a better, more wonderful world for which I am destined. Joy in the present is a foretaste of that future world.

"If we find ourselves with a desire that nothing in this world can satisfy, the most probable explanation is that we were made for another world."
C.S. Lewis

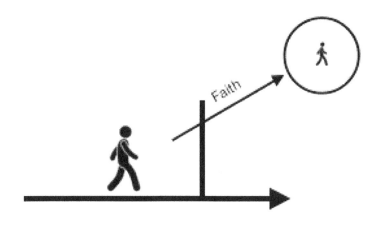

We are social creatures and know who we are because we exist in relationship with others. They give us feedback on who we are. So, for me to be me after death means I must be in relationship with others who are there also (see you soon, Gramps!)

That existence doesn't just happen. It is orchestrated by a God who has power over death and desires an eternal relationship with us. This is the ultimate relationship for all of us there and provides the true definition of who we are and provides ultimate meaning to our lives.

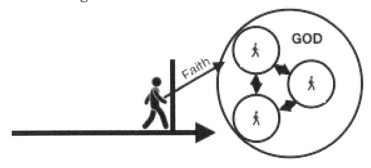

"He will wipe away every tear from their eyes; and there will no longer be any death; there will no longer be any mourning, or crying, or pain; the first things have passed away."

Revelation 21:4

"Death is only a launching into the region of the strange Untried; it is but the first salutation to the possibilities of the immense Remote, the Wild, the Watery, the Unshored."
Herman Melville

"Another world is not only possible, she is on her way. On a quiet day, I can her breathing."
Arundhati Roy

"End? No, the journey doesn't end here. Death is just another path, one that we all must take. The grey rain-curtain of this world rolls back, and all turns to silver glass, and then you see it. White shores, and beyond, a far green country under a swift sunrise."
J.R.R. Tolkien, *The Lord of the Rings*

AFTERTHOUGHT

Imagine a man who for all practical purposes represents the epitome of a perfect life as currently defined. He has a strong marriage to a beautiful woman, a son and a daughter who are mature and making their own impactful way through the world. He has a steady and secure job that financially more than provides for his family and allows him to take a big trip anywhere in the world every year. Things seem good.

But they're not. In comparison to the perfect impression of his life on the outside, inside he is an insecure mess. It's incongruous. His interior world is so crowded with doubts about himself that he becomes numb to the surroundings of his outside world. He will ride the train to work every morning without a thought to where he is or even to what he is doing. Unaware.

To compensate for such an incongruity, the man intensely regiments his life. He gets up at the same time every morning, eats the same breakfast, and takes the same train at the same time to the same job he has had for years. There, he goes through a similar routine, in the cubicle he has occupied for his whole tenure. When the workday is done, (he never puts in overtime; too unpredictable), he leaves at precisely the same moment the hands on the clock say he should.

From there, he rides the same train home, again oblivious to his surroundings. He is like an unconscious man, with no awareness of the details of his life, as he looks out the window at the passing landscape, despairing the disconnect he feels with that life.

He enters the door of his house, at a precise time, to find his stalwart wife waiting for him. It never varies. Then at a regularly scheduled dinner, he and his family eat. Talk there is superficial and mundane.

He waddles himself over to the same chair he has occupied since they owned the house and watches the same news, on the same broadcast, on at the same time every weekday. After some channel surfing and reading a book (he only likes mysteries), he settles himself in bed at the same moment he does every day, rain or shine.

One day he wakes up at the same time just as usual,

eats his same breakfast and begins his regimented routine, when suddenly something quite outside his of control intrudes. On the train platform, at a time he didn't plan or expect, the man suffers a major heart attack.

Here this man, who is so used to regularity and familiarity, is finding himself in a strange new world. He finds himself in an ambulance he has never ridden before, being worked on by people he has never met, being shuttled to a hospital he has never visited. His regimented, orderly life has become chaos and fear.

Arriving at the hospital, the man is secured to a gurney and whisked to the emergency room to be poked and prodded by people of whom he has no knowledge of.

Yet, on the quick journey from the back of the ambulance to the revolving doors of the ER, this normally unaware man becomes intensely interested and aware of his own hand.

He flips it. He can't believe he hasn't noticed how translucent and beautiful it is; The wrinkles on the knuckles, the coating on the fingernails (that he kept precisely trimmed), and the piano key like movement of its tendons. How could he have missed something so spectacular as his own hand!

He is put under anesthesia to become numb to the pain and reality of heart surgery for a few hours. When he groggily comes to, out of the stupor that was his medicine, he begins to take notice of the details of the room around him. He first sees a clock on the wall and remembers it is well past his usual bedtime. But he doesn't care. He is just happy to be alive. A heart attack can easily remind you how close to death you are.

After his recovery, he returns home, a different man. His wife is somehow more beautiful than he remembers. He deeply hugs his kids in a loving manner he has never done before. He eats ice cream for dessert. He sleeps in on the weekends.

More than that, he quits his job. One that was tedious and boring anyway. He takes a position with a company that doesn't pay as well but allows more flexibility in his daily schedule. He so wants to be there when his kids grow up and he so wants to experience life with the love of his life.

He sees the world with new eyes. It is like Rip Van

Winkle waking up. You remember the story of Rip Van Winkle. He falls asleep for 20 years and wakes up to a world that is strangely familiar but foreign all the same. It has moved on 20 years. It's the same world, but in many respects delightfully new.

So too, with the man on the train. His brief encounter with his own mortality woke him up to a new world. A world he always lived in but never was aware of. A delightfully new, intense, and beautiful world. Thank goodness, he thought, for this powerful engagement with death that provided a wakeup call. If only he had been aware of all this grandeur in life much, much earlier...

After all of that deep thought, I have arrived at this conclusion: When all is said and done, in spite of or because of what we may or may not do or think, it is just as likely as not that, for better or for worse, everything will turn out one way or another, sooner or later.

QUOTES

While so many people avoid talking or thinking about death, there are those through history that engage it head on. Here is a take on death and dying with quotes (I love quotes) by philosophers and comedians through the ages.

"Live as you would have wished to live when you are dying."
Christian Furchtegott Gellert

"You matter because you are you, and you matter to the end of your life. We will do all we can not only to help you die peacefully, but also to live until you die."
Dame Cicely Saunders

"The nearer she came to death, the more, by some perversity of nature, did she enjoy living."
Ellen Glasgow

"Some people are so afraid to die that they never begin to live."
Henry Van Dyke

"Life is pleasant. Death is peaceful. It's the transition that's troublesome."
Isaac Asimov

"Death helps us to see what is worth trusting and loving and what is a waste of time."
J. Neville Ward

"The question is not whether we will die, but how we will live."
Dr Joan Borysenko

"As a well-spent day brings happy sleep, so a life well used brings happy death."
Leonardo da Vinci

"Live as if you were to die tomorrow. Learn as if you were to live forever."
Mahatma Gandhi

"The fear of death follows from the fear of life. A man who lives fully is prepared to die at any time."
Mark Twain

"Forgive yourself before you die. Then forgive others."
Morrie Schwartz

"When you learn how to die, you learn how to live."
Morrie Schwartz

"Death is not the greatest loss in life. The greatest loss is what dies inside us while we live."
Norman Cousins

"Somebody should tell us, right at the start of our lives, that we are dying. Then we might live life to the limit, every minute of every day. Do it! I say. Whatever you want to do, do it now! There are only so many tomorrows."
Pope Paul VI

"… almost everything – all external expectations, all pride, all fear of embarrassment or failure – these things just fall away in the face of death, leaving only what is truly important. Remembering that you are going to die is the best way I know to avoid the trap of thinking you have something to lose. You are already naked.
There is no reason not to follow your heart."
Steve Jobs

"Every man dies – Not every man really lives."
William Ross Wallace

"Try as much as possible to be wholly alive, with all your might, and when you laugh, laugh like hell and when you get angry, get good and angry. Try to be alive. You will be dead soon enough."
William Saroyan

"I am not afraid of death, I just don't want to be there when it happens."
Woody Allen

"For mortals vanished from the day's sweet light. I shed no tear; rather I mourn for those who day and night live in death's fear."
Greek Epigram

"Life is about more that earning a living, and if you're not in the habit of thinking about it, you can end up middle-aged or even older and shocked to realize that your life seems empty."
Martha C. Nussbaum

"You can't do anything about the length of your life, but you can do something about its width and depth."
Evan Esar

"The tragic distortion is the when you avoid death, you also avoid life. And I don't know about you but I want to be there through all of it."
Joan Halifax

"When people know they are going to die, that last year is often the most loving, most conscious, and most caring - even under conditions of poor concentration, the side effects of medication, and so on. So don't wait to die until you die. Start practicing now."
Stephen Levine

ADDENDUM: LESSONS THE CORONAVIRUS, (OR THE AWARENESS OF MORTALITY), WANTS TO TEACH US

We were made for the struggle. The human race has shown an amazing ability to be resilient in tough times- we all wouldn't be here otherwise. Exposure to struggle, setbacks, and adversity can steel us to function better than expected with future challenges. It is similar to an inoculation that gives us the strength to resist future exposure to a disease.

Often the deepest joy comes from going through crisis and growing into a stronger, more vibrantly mortal person. Meaninglessness in life comes not from having too much pain, but from having too much pleasure. As much as we might not want it, inevitable adversity leads to a depth of meaning that can be garnered no other way.

And so here we are. We are currently living through what inevitably is an historic pandemic reminding us of our mortality. The coronavirus is another way of describing the awareness of our mortality. Corona virus = awareness of our mortality.

Becoming a stronger person because of adversity and setbacks is one of the deeper satisfactions in life. However, in order to thrive in the midst of them, we must make a choice. You can either choose to let the situation shackle you with weakness and insecurity or you can choose to lean forward into the headwinds of the storm and find the strength to walk on through.

Commitment is the choice to give up choices. When confronted with a difficult situation you must make the choice to give up the choice to give in. It must not even be an option in your mind. You must have a whole-hearted resolve to face the difficulty full on and accept the pain that comes along with it. It's tough though. And there's the kicker.

The weaker response of giving in to adversity is the easier way. That's why so many people wallow through life. Giving up rather than getting up is a weakened response that doesn't take much effort. It's also surrendering to self-pity and inactivity- the enemies of resolve.

Getting up from tough times takes courage and strength. It's a battle, and a tough one at that. It's the wounds of that battle that leads to wisdom.

I finished writing this book about a month before the coronavirus truly went pandemic. I didn't realize the awareness of our mortality would be so close up and personal this widely and this soon; that we would be facing such a huge human crisis.

The virus has forced us globally to become aware of our mortality in a way that is unprecedented.
Again, death is the most relevant topic on the planet and has many lessons to teach us. Hopefully these lessons will also be the realities of a new normal when things settle down.

So, the historic coronavirus pandemic (or the awareness of our mortality) has <u>lessons</u> it wants to teach you. These might also be surprising new realities when this all shakes out. Coronavirus wants you to:

Lower your expectations

According to a report on life satisfaction in the developed world, Denmark is the happiest country on earth. The reason? Denmark has low expectations. They don't expect a whole lot to be positive so anything that hints of something good elevates their mood.

The United States came in 11th and falling. Our happiness is very much tied to good news. We generally have high expectations and are often disappointed by the negative news that inevitably comes. So, we become bummed. Given the day and age we live in and the pervasive malaise that hangs over our lives, life satisfaction for us has to rise, right? We'll see. It's getting easier and easier to lower our expectations. That might be good news.

Handcraft each day to your liking, for it truly is unique.

For many, being asked to stay at home has provided the impetus to be creative with what you do with each day. It also re-establishes the wonder and beauty of home, wherever and whatever that is.

Grow deep through pain, since pain deepens us for growth.

Like it or not, the most powerful lessons are forged through pain and suffering. Lessons learned through the crucible of pain lead to wisdom. Wisdom comes from scar tissue. Do you know what I mean when I say that? Life has to kick you down only for you to get back up again wounded but stronger and wiser by it.

Live with ambiguity

Ask yourself this question:

"Is your life out of control?" Well, if it isn't, it ought to be…

Social scientists have done extensive research on the human response to ambiguity and uncertainty in our lives. They have discovered that one of our defense mechanisms for protecting against the fear of chaos is the illusion of control.

Control is merely an illusion. But we persist in living by it every day.

Think of the simple act of activating an elevator. We pushed the button and wait for its arrival. But what we do if it doesn't arrive in our perceived time frame? We press the button again. The illusion of control.

We often attempt to control traffic jams. If you're like me, I play traffic jams like chess matches. I strategize moves and counter moves in an attempt to beat the jam and foil its traps.

But alas, I find myself usually more irritated and late as usual. The illusion of control.
But we persist in guiding our lives by its illusion.

We can't help ourselves. We are good modern, Western, scientific people and we prefer to be in control – but it is in reality a mirage that fails to provide the needed resources for our journey. Particularly during this awareness of our mortality.

A characteristic of the pandemic we find ourselves in at the moment is Ambiguity. It is uncertain and disconcerting. We don't know precisely where we are headed, and we have no control as to how to get there.

So, we need to relax during tough times. Let go of control. Embrace uncertainty. Gather some dear friends, drink some good wine, and laugh at your predicaments.

"If we all couldn't laugh, we would all go insane"

Be a kinder person, it's contagious

You've seen how swiftly the awareness of our mortality can spread throughout the world. Kindness will spread even faster and have far greater results.

Let days go by without regret, you can't have them back anyway

Give up your hope that you will have a better past.

Don't plan too many years in advance. They haven't come to life yet.

Being Vibrantly Mortal means there is an awareness of how fleeting and fragile life is and there is no guarantee tomorrow will come with the "certainty" of our plans. One of the biggest lesson's mortality has taught me, is that sacrificing my present life while waiting for my future life is futile.

Be a Deviant, for the world is our home for now

Be a Deviant. In school you were always told to sit down and keep in place. Any unexpected outbursts were punished, and the "naughtiest" kids were the ones always in detention. We were taught to play by the rules and keep in line. You were often told to color inside the lines and told bears aren't purple.

Think of Lego, the plastic building blocks that have entertained generations of children. It used to be you would just receive the blocks and were left to your own devices to build what was in your head. Now a days, you get your Lego blocks along with a multipage guidebook telling you exactly what you need to do to build the ship or plane or whatever. Imagination gave way to instruction.

Yet, it is coloring outside the lines and not playing by the rules that often lead to major breakthroughs. It is throwing away the instruction manual and venturing beyond the step by step. To be a deviant means venturing outside your comfort zone and the way things are to bring renewed hope.

Listen to the Beatles, and discover true craftsmanship

I am been a bit obsessive over the music of the Beatles. It is incredible and I have not tired from listening to their songs over and over again. It has been many decades since their breakup and the quality and endurance of their songs remains.

I got to thinking what makes the Beatles such an enduring band. More specifically what has given their songs such staying power? I doubt in forty-one years we will still be listening to Britney Spears.

So, here are the reasons…

> -The very high quality of each song. I am discovering that listening to the Beatles is best done with headphones. There you pick up the variety of instruments layered over the various tracks. Very well done and worth listening to often. There is a richness to their delivery.

> -The vibrant creativity brought to the songwriting. Who can listen to their album *Revolver* without an awareness of the band's creative and imaginative experimentation? It propelled them from the "bubble gum" pop of their early years (still great songs by the way)

into a more imaginative and experimental phase in their songwriting

-The mature movement toward engagement with life. The Beatles told stories in their songs and narrated the exuberance (Ob -li-de, Ob-li-da) as well as the angst (Eleanor Rigby; A day in the life). What is music if it can't address the human condition?

I think there are lessons here for our lives and the leaving of an enduring legacy.

-Live life with excellence. For us this is really an issue of integrity; do your inside values match your outward actions and do you do everything with an incomparable example?

-Live life creatively. We are, in the words of J.R.R. Tolkien, sub-creators of the one Creator God. We were made to embed our unique contribution into the world.

-Live life fully and honestly. We must not shy away from the muck and the grime of life but rather to engage it fully with joy or sorrow.

After all, you can't have one without the other. I prefer to hang out with people who have been wounded by life and have learned to bounce back and thrive with wisdom at their core.

The Beatles have endured, and I believe will continue to do so because of their dogged pursuit of quality, their continued imaginative exploration in their songwriting, and an honest, straightforward engagement with life in all its complexity.

I think we can endure throughout the width and breadth and depth of our own mortal lives with excellence, imagination, and an honest engagement.

Read more books, they make us more human

Maybe stay at home orders will compel us all to get back to reading as an extended activity.

Take a nap every day. The stats are out on its benefits

A nap can be like a sabbath- a reminder that we don't have to strive all the time to make a living or mold ourselves to our culture's definition. It can be form of resistance against the modern world.

Don't settle for mediocre coffee, make the buzz worthwhile

Support your local coffee roaster. It's good not only for the palate but for the neighborhood. Make the buzz worthwhile.

Exercise your soul. Meditate daily.

Nurture the soul. This is best done in contemplation and silence. It is very hard in our noisy world to try sitting silently for 20 minutes. Let any thought that comes your way to flow along out of your consciousness so that you can be fully present with the eternal.

Live outside your comfort zone

When you stretch yourself, you never bound back the same shape again. When I went to help out in Boulder during historic flooding, my car got stuck in the mud. It was literally like driving into quicksand. I had to hire a tow truck to bail me out.

Life can often feel like quicksand. We sink and feel

stuck. Here are some of the causes that get us stuck in life:

-lack of purpose. Ancient mariners guided their ships by sexton. This devise would cue up to the north star or other fixed position and give them a bearing of where they were at. But what if the night sky changed position every night? You would be lost. We often live our lives without a north star to follow. What is your north star, your purpose and reason for being?

-lack of commitment. A good definition of commitment is "making the choice to give up choices". Since we live in a day and age with a bombardment of choices, it's getting harder and hard to commit. This lack of commitment keeps us "wishy-washy" and unable to settle in on any one thing. Make a choice and stick with it.

-lack of movement. The doldrums are lulls at sea where there is absolutely no wind. It is a dead zone, stranding many sailing ships of old. We can find ourselves in the doldrums with little or no movement toward a goal or living life forward. To get moving again takes concerted effort. It's just getting started on whatever task or goal you have set out for yourself. Getting started is the hardest part.

-lack of direction. I once got lost hiking. It was a scary experience. I lost my direction and paid the price. I got my bearings back when I ran across a trail marker giving me direction to where I needed to go next to get back.

Coming out of your comfort zone means paying attention to 2.1 markers:

1) where you are,

2) where you want to be, and

.1) the very next step to get you there.

Always be open to joy

We have the right to life and liberty and the pursuit of happiness. Happiness in and of itself is not a right, it's a lifelong pursuit. Yet it seems so evasive. We think we got it and it slips through our hands. It's like trying to catch a butterfly in a net. Fleeting.

Joy, on the other hand, is deeper than happiness and

pursues us. Happiness relies on circumstance, joy does not. Joy can capture us in the most unlikely of situations. When things seem at their worse, joy can break through. Though I pursue happiness, I'm grateful that joy relentlessly pursues and captures me.

Use obstacles for growth

If we wait to take a trip until all the lights are green, we'll never go. Life is a series of stops and starts. It never follows a predictable, barrier free path. So, when you find your path is blocked, realize the following dynamics:

-When you encounter a barrier blocking your path, remember they are an inevitable part of life and need to be taken care of.

-There are always alternative paths you can take to get back on the path. Sometimes those diversions provide surprising adventures.

-You could do the hard work of removing the barrier, taking the time needed to go through it. Doing this creates a plan and develops strength.

Either way, when your path is blocked, the obstacles provide responses for our growth.

Use Endings as Beginnings

I read an article somewhere with the title, "What is it about Toy Story 3 that makes grown men cry?" The movie had just come out and was getting plenty of accolades. I went and watched it with the title of the article in mind.

It's true. A pixelated cartoon made me cry. At its core, the movie was about letting go and moving on. Specifically, letting go of childhood and moving on to the adult world. Andy, the main character, was packing up his life and moving on to college.

There is a scene where Andy's mom is standing in his now empty room. The wallpaper with clouds is now devoid of posters. His toys have all been packed up. She stands there for a moment and realizes the pain of letting go. I cried. I just dropped my son off at college. There is the bittersweet moment of letting someone we love, move out of childhood and into adulthood, or from life to death.

I stood in my son's empty room. Some shoes of his are there, and some shirts are hanging in the closet. Remnants of his life at home. I cried. Those tears contained both sadness and joy. I have to let him go into his newfound life outside of his childhood home.

That's the thing about endings. They are relay stations to the next moment in life. They move us forward into new beginnings. If we let them, they help grow us up and move us on. Funerals are great rituals for compelling us to let go and move on.

Be grateful always

I have a gratitude app on my smart phone. It just pinged me that I haven't been grateful for anything in the last 3 days. I have been, I just haven't written it down. I need to. It keeps me grounded. Gratitude is essential for the following reasons:

> -A friend of mine, known as the "Grateful Dad," intentionally lived a grateful life for one year, journaled it, and found that his business and life had exploded with growth. Gratitude provides enrichment to our lives.

-No matter the situation, there is always something to be grateful for. It could even be for the tough ordeal that made you a stronger human being.

-Gratitude is contagious. Taking up an "attitude of gratitude" spreads not only to your own life on a regular basis but is caught by those around you. They will feel appreciated. Who doesn't want that?

-Like an oil well, gratitude breaks through the crusty topsoil and taps into the valuable elixir below. The subsequent geyser is worth millions. Valuable indeed.

-Gratitude points us to the smallest wonders of life; the laugh of a baby, the work of the ant, the growth of the flower. With gratitude everything seems charged with eternity

We can often develop amnesia for the good things in our lives. Gratitude keeps us focused on the current elements to celebrate. It keeps negativity at bay. Living a grateful life is a sacred trust. It sees all of life as reason to celebrate even if you don't necessarily feel like it at the time. I have friends with a diagnosis of cancer who are the most grateful people I know. For them, every moment in life is something to be grateful for.

We all want to go to bed in the evening and believe we have done a good job. It's a bonus to find fulfillment in our vocations and hobbies. Heck, it's nice to get a pat on the back if not from someone else then at least from our own selves. The task is challenging and requires skill. We are stimulated toward growth. The following are the psychological components of Gratification:

-<u>Concentration</u>. A focus on the task at hand

-<u>Clear goals</u>. We can measure our progress and completion with immediate feedback.

-<u>Deep, effortless involvement</u>. Some call this being in the "flow".

-<u>A Sense of Control</u>. We can participate in the outcome

-<u>Sense of Self</u>. The ego gives way to gift.

-<u>Time stops</u>. This is when time "flies"

Be grateful this day in all that you do…

Write your narrative with a different script

His eyes met the eyes of his betrayer on the battlefield. What little life was left in him seeped away like a deflated balloon; limp, lifeless, and empty. How could comrades betray him so blatantly? He had put his trust in them and relied on them to defeat the enemy. What the hell?

In the movie, *Braveheart*, William Wallace, the leader of a guerrilla movement to free Scotland in the 1300's was despondent. Battles had been tough but victorious. To deal the final blow to English tyranny, Wallace needed the Scottish nobles as allies. He relied on them, trusted this alliance with his life. It was the only way.

Yet, in the heat of battle, the nobles aided the enemy. Wallace lost all vitality for victory. His elan for battle depleted. If the nobles could so easily dismiss the mission to free Scotland, what hope was there?

As the reality of the betrayal became evident. William Wallace laid prone on the battlefield, giving in to the enemy. It was a white flag of surrender.

You could see it in his eyes. They were pale and lifeless. The light in them extinguished. He gave into defeat.

Life is a battle. Skirmishes occur every day. We can so often feel betrayed or worse yet, abandoned.

We all live by a script, socialized in us from the beginning, with a message: you are worth it or you are not. The later script becomes a narrative of defeat. Decisions are made, relationships are forged, life is lived with the undercurrent of defeat. Victory seems elusive, so foreign to our experience that we continue on deeply despondent.

Don't live by the narrative of defeat. Overcome it with the following scripts.

> -The script of value
> You might remember the Saturday Night Live skit where a therapist was counseling Michael Jordan. His mantra for him was, "I'm good enough, I'm strong enough, and doggone it, I'm worth it!" All kidding aside, and at the risk of sounding "flu-flu", that mantra isn't too shabby to help us see ourselves as valuable.

-<u>The script of success</u>

I'm not much of a law of attraction guy. But I do believe our approach to success has ramifications. If you live by a narrative of defeat, you live feeling unsuccessful. Like attracts like, and soon success seems ethereal. If you don't believe you're successful, you won't be, in your mind anyway. It's also critical that you know what your definition of success is.

-<u>The script of maturity</u>

To live life fully, we must live it with maturity. That is, drawing from the wellspring of wisdom from your life, you can approach life with big boy/girl pants.

Maturity is tough, it only comes to fruition through life lived and learned. To refuse to learn is an invitation to immaturity and defeat.

Never take relationships for granted. Ever.

It goes without saying that relationships are important. We are social creatures and know ourselves through the feedback of a community. Even in the best of circumstances, maintaining relationships that thrive takes a lot of work and savvy.

It doesn't help, then, that our culture conspires against our relationships. The following three factors are ever present in the ether of our lives (whether we know it or not) and impede good relationships:

-Narcissism.
You might remember the Greek myth of Narcissus. He was renowned for his beauty and was especially prideful. The Greek god Nemesis exploited those qualities and had Narcissus fall in love with his own image reflected in a pool of water. He died lonely and infatuated only with himself.

Think about your consumer culture. It plays off the narcissus in each of us. It wants us to believe we are the center of the universe, touting individualism and unconcerned about a reality beyond our private lives.

-Pragmatism
This is an overly dependent belief that only that which works is worth pursuing. What is true is what works. If your relationship works, great. If it doesn't, jettison it along with all the other effluvia that doesn't work in your life.

It states your worth lies in achievement. Value lies in being practical. There is much to pragmatism that is good. Many of the good things we enjoy today come from pragmatism. The issue though, is our pragmatic tendency to place value on ourselves and others from what we do rather than who we are (our authentic self).

-<u>Freneticism</u>
This is unbridled restlessness. We flit to and fro, hither and yonder at light speeds in a vain attempt to get on top of life. The faster we go, we believe, the more success will be assured. An excuse so many of us use is that of busyness. The consequence is, of course, the depletion of a deep, interior life. The speed of life only propels us off the surface of life, like a stone skipped across water.

Relationships flourish when we are more concerned with the other in our midst than we are with ourselves. Relationships flourish when we know each other at the core of their identity; their heart. Relationships flourish when we slow down long enough to share unfettered time with family and friends.

Thank the awareness of our mortality for that.

Live again

The man stood on the bridge intent on killing himself.
His life was in tatters. His business owed a debt it
couldn't repay and was tanking fast. He had just blown
up at his family. He was in an existential mid-life crisis.
He looked over his life; his mundane, disappointing
life, and didn't like what he saw. Not one bit. It was
the end of the line. The man was desperate.

He jumped. He suddenly found himself in the
netherworld between life and death, miraculously able
to see what life would be like if he didn't exist. It was a
unique predicament.

As he wandered through the scenes of his life, the
people and places that meant so much to him, he was
confronted with a deep sense of awe. Life without him
in it, he discovered, had profound repercussions. He
realized, in ways he couldn't explain, that he
completely missed the wonder of his every day,
ordinary life, right there in front of his nose all the

time. He suddenly became very desperate for life, his former life; his ordinary, harsh, and magnificent life. The man made his way to the edges of his deathly existence and found himself on the bridge once again. This time was different. He wanted to live and not die. Like a geyser that erupts under pressure, the man desperately prayed to live again. "I want to live again" he desperately implored. "I want to live again".

That plot line from the perennial holiday classic, "It's a Wonderful Life", speaks volumes about the story of our life as it unfolds, with plot twists both harsh and rewarding. Life can be so damn difficult that we can miss the magic of our ordinary lives.

My battle with bipolar disorder has zapped much enjoyment and full engagement from the youthful years of my life. I loathe its companionship. I spent most of my time protecting my heart from stress and strain for fear they would lead to the terror of bone jarring depression. The kind that hits you in the stomach with a fist that hurts so deeply you bleed despair. Let me tell you, you do not want to go there. So, I stayed above the fray of life by being benign. That will keep me safe.

My career has never really taken off. I'm a very good public speaker, yet I've rarely used that gift consistently over my life. Since speaking before an audience is a vulnerable act, I wonder if I've avoided even that to keep depression from triggering its pain. I just don't know. Maybe.

I want to live again.

I want to feel giddy holding hands with my wife. I want to "date" my daughters whenever I can. I want to speak and impact lives. I want to live with exuberance and gratitude every day that comes my way. I no longer want to protect my heart with impenetrable armor. I want to be vulnerable. I want to deepen my faith in God. I want to be the best friend I can possibly be. I want to drink more craft beer.

You may have lost someone very close to you to cancer. You might have been laid off from a job you thought would last forever. Maybe you struggle with an invisible disability that's drained a lot of your resolve. You might be turning 50 and regret much of your life. If your marriage is in deep trouble, it can live again. Are you starting a new career? You can live again in it. You can live again no matter what. Like a phoenix rising from the ashes, your life can emerge with a beauty and wonder you can't imagine.

Let the reality of death motivate you to live again too. Begin exploring what living again is all about; how to live again in your family; how to live again in your job; how to live again with your family; heck, even how to live again laughing so hard milk comes out your nose.

I'm not sure where my explorations will take me, but I can guarantee you one thing- they won't be dead any longer.

What are some ways you found to live again?

Be open to failure

I had a speaking gig a year ago. I left feeling good about the material and my delivery of it. Yet the reviews that came in were the worst I ever received as a speaker. Not horrible, but still. It was obvious I failed. The audience wasn't engaged, and I apparently wasn't very dynamic (the first time for that feedback). I was deflated.

It took some time, but I came out of it and learned some powerful lessons. After all, the issue isn't whether you failed, but rather, did you learn anything from it and were you able to move on in constructive ways. I believe there are four lessons to learn from our moments of failure to move us on to a richer life.

-Lesson One: Success often starts with failure
This sounds counter-intuitive. Yet, you never know what success is unless you've experienced failure. The two go hand in hand. They're partners together in defining a human life.

Failure lights the fuse to the explosion of success. Failure makes success that much sweeter. Failure creates the "scar tissue" that leads to wisdom. It is wisdom that makes your success beneficial to the world and keeps you tempered with humility.

-Lesson Two: Failure opens you up to honest improvement
There is no sugar-coating failure. It slaps us in often brutally honest and revealing ways. After my poor review I had to stop and assess why I received it. It laid me bare to myself. I could have chosen to let it fester by never dealing with the

failure. Or I could engage it as an ally in my improvement. I chose the latter.

I couldn't make excuses for myself. I had to take a deep look at the moment and assess what I could learn to be better next time. After all, it's easy to rest on our laurels. Sometimes the thing we do best becomes detrimental when we cease to improve it. We can rely too easily on our strengths that it hinders us and can rely on it too flippantly to get things done.

-<u>Lesson Three: Failure integrates you with all human beings</u>

I shared my failure above because I know you've been there. I didn't share anything you don't understand. I'm not the only one.

It's always good to know you're in good company. Abraham Lincoln failed in business numerous times. Every person alive today including every person that ever lived has been a failure at some point. It's a broken world after all. It's when we begin to fuse our failures to a learning curve that the world seems whole again.

-<u>Lesson Four: Failure strengthens your resolve</u>.

Many people give up when they fail. Jens Voigt, a world class bicycle racer and fixture at the Tour de France, had a horrible crash that shattered most of the bones in his face. He later wrote an article that impressed the importance of getting back on the bike. Many young riders, he pointed out, fail to race again because they can't get back on the bike after a crash.

Failure can sometimes feel like a crash that leaves us wounded and afraid. Regardless of the intensity of our failure we need to strengthen our resolve and get back on the bike.

Failure acts as a sage for our life. We just need to be open to the lessons it imparts.

Always let Love run wild

There are a lot of graduation speeches out there. You know, all the standard stuff about seizing the moment and creating your future. Blah, Blah, Blah.

The best one in my opinion was given by the principle of a High School. She talked about three important words they must never forget as they venture forth from the hallowed halls of school.

I'm not going to tell you what they were just yet. I'm cruel that way. Yes, they were powerful. Yes, they were transcendent. But her three words, heck, any three words when taken together pale in comparison to three words together. I believe they make all the difference in the world. Don't get me wrong. I'm not some guy who thinks I have a corner on the market for three words. I've just not found any that fully trump these three.

These three words have encouraged people throughout history to move through incredible difficulty and accomplish amazing things. These three words are the core of every significant relationship in life and play a role in peripheral relationships as well. These three words have the weight and wonder of eternity behind them. These three words are sometimes the only ones left to be uttered at the death bed of a loved one. They help to lighten murky thoughts and enliven despairing moments.

Taken together, they stand on their own. These three words together will endure after your physical self is long gone. Not to worry though. These three words will propel you and your life beyond the physical here and now and transport you to the eternal there and then. They are the basis of joy.

Ready for 'em? Here they are:

Love. Never. Fails.

The love I'm talking about isn't the fleeting infatuation that sparks love. It is a wizened love forged over time and sustained in monotony. It's the kind of love I receive from my wife every day; a persistent and genuine love.

> -<u>A relentless love stays no matter what</u>. Even in the midst of the tremendous strains that can befall a marriage, love stays in the promise of a strengthened resolve to work it out together.

> -<u>A relentless love isn't afraid to expose vulnerabilities</u>. To expose oneself, warts and all, is to invite critique and criticism. Love embraces the foibles of the other and redeems them together.

> -<u>A relentless love tells it like it is</u>. Things are

never hunky dory in a relationship all the time. Hurting the other person happens.

Sometimes we don't even know we are doing it. Love shares the hurt and brings a balm that heals.

-<u>A relentless love is a mystery</u>. To try and figure out why love exists and turn it into a system of tips and principles is to diminish its power. There is more to it than meets the eye or is confined in the mind.

-<u>A relentless love is frustrating</u>. Relationships are messy. Sometimes the action of the other can create a reality that defies expectations and leave you scratching your head. Love is open to change and works out the disparate expectations.

-<u>A relentless love is a gift and a joy</u>. It isn't easy but it's the only force on earth stronger than a diamond and softer than a pillow. It holds out hope and is forever evolving to meet the changing dynamics of relationship and committed to the long term. What a joy!

Excuse me now. I have a good craft IPA waiting for me with a plan of sitting in the sun with the love of my life.

Don't be a Visitor

As time moves on, and I reflect back on life, there's an urgency to live life fully; no messing around.
So…

> *"…when it's over, I want to say: all my life*
> *I was a bride married to amazement*
>
> *I was a bridegroom, taking the world into my arms*
>
> *When it's over, I don't want to wonder if I have*
> *made of my life something particular, and real.*
>
>
> *I don't want to find myself sighing and frightened*
> *or full of argument.*
>
> *I don't want to end up simply having visited this*
> *world."*
> **Mary Oliver**

Fight the uphill battle

I read a fascinating op-ed in the New York Times about John Borling. John was a prisoner in the notorious prison known as the "Hanoi Hilton" in North Korea. He was subjected to intense torture and often complete isolation. It was futile, yet he managed to grit through the experience and the subsequent failures after his liberation to learn the power of dogged perseverance.

A story that has stuck with John is Camus's "Myth of Sisyphus". In it, the hero is condemned by the gods to push a rock up a hill without ever making it fully to the top. It would roll down to the bottom and had to be pushed back up the hill again with the same results over and over again. What's interesting is the hero is ultimately a happy man.

Happiness is found in coming to terms with futility. That sounds counter intuitive, but in a broken world life is a series of hills we are asked to push a rock up. Unlike Sisyphus we make it to the top and see the rock roll down the other side, only to be lodged at the bottom of another hill. We push it back up and over and onto another hill and another and another.

Coming to terms with the fact that life is a series of uphill battles requiring tough, tiring tasks is the first step to peace. Not to mention tough mental fortitude, and the hope that we will, someday, conquer that final hill- our own death.

Unleash the best of yourself

To live with death requires that we be as vibrant in our emotional, physical, and spiritual lives as we can possibly be. Yet we come up against a force that holds us down and prevents us from thriving. It's called suppression. Suppression has been the cause of ulcers, mental issues, insecurities, and ineffectiveness throughout all of human history.

Quite simply put, suppression is the holding down of who we really are and a folding in on ourselves by outside influences, memories, and even well- meaning people. We seem to spend the first forty years of our life living out what we believe others want us to be and spend the last forty years living out who we were created to be in the first place.

My son is a fantastic swimmer. But for two years he was stuck in a pattern that produced the same times in his races. He wasn't getting any faster and couldn't break the "barrier" of time that he wanted to succeed. There was no evidence of improvement and it was getting him down. Two years is a long time.

I'm very proud of him. He could have suppressed his talent by telling himself that he was "washed up", that his days of swimming excellence were over. He didn't. He hung in there, working through the agony of not improving his times, and bounced back. He knew there was something inside him that would propel him forward. His hard work confirmed what he knew- he was fast and capable.

He now has broken through the barrier and has risen to a new level of competence. He unleashed the best of himself.

Thrive

Scientists in the Arctic have bored down through two miles of ice and discovered ancient lakes that lie below. To their surprise they found evidence of simple microbial life thriving there. In spite of harsh, inhospitable conditions, life found a way to excel and thrive.

In the seemingly cold, harsh conditions of our world here on the surface, life, too finds a way to excel and thrive. Here are the ways life does that:

-It excels and thrives when you deliver impeccable service because your client matters.

-It excels and thrives when you volunteer at a soup kitchen.

-It excels and thrives when you wrap your arms around a hurting child.

-It excels and thrives when you find the humor in the absurd.

-It excels and thrives when you make a delicious meal to share with friends.

-It excels and thrives when you say no to unsavory offers.

-It excels and thrives when you stand up against teasing and bullying.

-It excels and thrives when you post compelling,

positive entries on social media.

-It excels and thrives when you admit who you are matters to others.

Life happens every moment. It excels and thrives, however, when you harness it with love, compassion, and action.

Bottom line: Even in the awareness of our mortality, Life happens! It excels and thrives thru you.

Don't wallow in the swamp

We all start out each day with the best of intentions. No one wakes up in the morning and declares "I'm going to botch today!" But things come up and our human weaknesses show through. Not every time. But there are times.

It's especially tough when you have been doing something over a period of time and it just isn't doing it. It's not working. That wasn't your intention starting out, but it happened. It might be a business venture. Dating. A hobby. Hair style. Career.

Someone said the definition of "insanity" is doing the

same thing over and over again and getting the same result. It's a "stuckness." A mire. A bog.

I'm reminded of the movie "The Shining" starring Jack Nicholson. His character Jack spends an entire winter alone with his family in a large hotel. He is tasked with taking care of it in the off season.

Throughout the course of the movie he continues to be more and more possessed by the evil atmosphere of the hotel. His wife suspects something is up and checks in on what Jack was doing all this time.

She thought he was writing a novel but instead he typed over and over again on hundreds of pages, "All work and no play makes Jack a dull boy". He was doing something, getting nowhere, and going mad.

So, what do you do when what you're doing isn't doing it? It's a tough question to answer. We tend to stay in a familiar situation (however crappy) than risk moving toward an unknown, and possibly, better reality. It's called "Ambiguity Aversion".

It can possess you and keep you in your place. When things aren't working out it's easy to wallow in the swamp. It's tougher to take a step out into the unknown and move to higher ground.

So, what do you do when what you're doing isn't doing it? You can start by taking the following actions.

-Shake up your routine. There is a sign on a road in Alaska that reads, "Rough road next thirty miles, choose your rut wisely".
Shaking it up can be as simple as brushing your teeth with your left hand instead of your right or taking a different route to work. You'll be surprised how powerful a simple change in routine can add luster to the day.

-Leave bad habits behind. This can be extremely hard to do. Habits get deeply engrained in our psyches. There are good habits and bad habits. Determine which ones are which by monitoring how you feel when you engage in them.

Bad habits don't enrich who you are. Rather they prevent you from being what you truly can be. You feel weakened; stalled. It's tough to go cold turkey so a steady diminishment of bad habits is the best way to. Be intentional in their erosion from your life.

-<u>Behave differently</u>. We act our way into a new way of being. Cognitive Behavioral Therapy is very effective. It focuses not only on relinquishing cognitive distortions, but also on behaving in effective ways. The two taken together can change a person's outlook and way of life.

-<u>Relax and Risk</u>. The two go together. Think of life as a series of trapeze swings. In order to make the jump to the next swing and the one after and the one after that is to relax your grip on the bar and then risk the jump to capture the new situation presenting itself. You'll have a few trapeze moments in life.
Take advantage of capturing each one.

-<u>Alter the dream</u>. This isn't killing the dream. It's heart breaking to hear Fantine's haunting expression of loss in *Les Misérables* when she sings in the signature song, "life has killed the dream I dreamed". Rather, it is moving toward the dream using an alternate route.

You need to be willing and able to switch directions away from dead ends. It can be tough and seem like the dream is dead. But a new direction often reignites passion.

Life is too short to wallow in the swamp.

Live beyond your potential

Time goes by swiftly, often upending our good intentions and leaving us with nothing but potential. Everyone has potential. The problem is, potential doesn't really get you anywhere. It's easy to default to the potential position- "I have the potential to be a great speaker"; or "My potential to be an artist has never been higher." Potential is a subtle form of making excuses for inactivity. I've written about it before. Must be a theme in my life.

An awareness of our mortality encourages you to move beyond potential to action. After all, you don't feel your way into a new way of being, you act your way into a new way of being. So, let's get off our butts of potentiality and get into the game. To do that you must overcome two behavioral barriers to living a full life:

-<u>Cowering</u>– Cowering is a weak response to the stresses and strains in life. Rather than boldly go where no one has gone before, we crouch down on our knees, arms crossed above our heads to lessen the blows as we acquiesce to the challenges in life. We stay put because we don't have the confidence to move ahead. If you say, "I can never do that", you're cowering. Find out what you can do instead and courageously see it through.

-<u>Wallowing</u>– Wallowing is staying in place while doing things that look like progress. It's often called "spinning your wheels". It's the avoidance of making decisions and committing to any one thing. Busyness is wallowing. We stay put by being busy all the time. Busy doing what? Have you found yourself saying "I can't do that, I'm way too busy." You're wallowing. Have a purpose and stop being so busy.

I hate to admit it but I'm really good at cowering and wallowing. I have to remember they don't just affect me but friends and family also. They deserve a person who is courageous and decisive. Someone who is vibrant. Besides, in light of my mortality, being vibrant is a much more adventurous way to live.

Be a complete person

It begs the question: how does your information stand out among all the other information that is swirling around your brain like a tornado? In addition, you might think you have nothing of importance that people would be interested in anyway. To that I say, "Poppycock!" to the following misconceptions (even I can get into the Dutch swing of things!).

-It's a lot of poppycock to think your life experience isn't important. It is. Your story is yours alone and has significance for others.

-It's a lot of poppycock to think what you do doesn't matter. It does. Your vocation is making a difference whether you know it or not.

-It's a lot of poppycock to think who you are isn't good enough. You're the only one of your kind.

I'm not much for rah, rah, siss, boom, bah you can be

and do anything you want mumble jumble. It too often lets people down. What you can do is be as complete a person as is possible for you, warts and all, writing your life story and planting yourself firmly in the place you are planted. You have something to offer that others will be hungry to embrace. As a friend of mine, a former Disney Imagineer, McNair Wilson says,

"If you don't do you, you won't get done, and the world will be less because of it."

Develop your mental fortitude

There have been athletes at the Olympic games coming in as heavy favorites to win the gold. Some, however, didn't attain it. It is in that moment of defeat that an athlete really proves their mettle. It's called mental fortitude and it is critical to any endeavor in sports and in life.

Building mental fortitude is tough. I entail daily practice in capturing your thoughts, sifting through them, and focusing on the ones that will make you stronger.

Think of all the events in your life that don't go your

way. It could be a diagnosis, a missed field goal, a layoff, or any other number of things. Kicking in the mental fortitude that you have strengthened over time will make you a true champion indeed. Here are some suggestions for a good mental "workout".

-<u>Meditation</u>: Monks who spend time in meditation controlling their thoughts actually have physical changes in their brainwaves that help them stay calm. It only takes 20 minutes a day, of silence to make a big difference. The tough part is breaking away from the megaphone of noise in our lives.

-<u>Feedback</u>: Athletes have teammates that help them keep things in perspective. They are encouraged to stay strong, reminding them that they are world class athletes and errors happen. Seek outside eyes on your life to keep a check on your perspective.

-<u>Awareness</u>: Some call this being fully present in the moment. Concentrating on living each moment with deliberation helps strengthen your participation in life and keeps you grounded in what is important. Take the next ten minutes and concentrate on nothing else other than what you are doing in that time. Write down what that felt like.

Cognitive distortions are thoughts that cause individuals to perceive reality inaccurately. The following are a list of those distortions adapted from a book by David Burns and Aaron T. Bech entitled *Feeling Good: The New Mood Therapy* and listed as given from the positivepsychology.com website.

I myself have shrunk these distortions down to a card I can keep in my wallet as well as taped to my bathroom mirror for reference. I refer to these every day. Beyond meditation, visiting these distortions is the most important exercise in my day to keep up good mental health.

1. <u>All-or-Nothing Thinking / Polarized Thinking</u>

Also known as "Black-and-White Thinking," this distortion manifests as an inability or unwillingness to see shades of gray. In other words, you see things in terms of extremes – something is either fantastic or awful, you believe you are either perfect or a total failure.

2. Overgeneralization

This sneaky distortion takes one instance or example and generalizes it to an overall pattern. For example, a student may receive a 'C' on one test and conclude that she is stupid and a failure.

Overgeneralizing can lead to overly negative thoughts about yourself and your environment based on only one or two experiences.

3. Mental Filter

Similar to overgeneralization, the mental filter distortion focuses on a single negative piece of information and excludes all the positive ones. An example of this distortion is one partner in a romantic relationship dwelling on a single negative comment made by the other partner and viewing the relationship as hopelessly lost, while ignoring the years of positive comments and experiences. The mental filter can foster a decidedly pessimistic view of everything around you by focusing only on the negative.

4. Disqualifying the Positive

On the flip side, the "Disqualifying the Positive" distortion acknowledges positive experiences but rejects them instead of embracing them.

For example, a person who receives a positive review at work might reject the idea that they are a competent employee and attribute the positive review to political correctness, or to their boss simply not wanting to talk about their employee's performance problems.

This is an especially malignant distortion since it can facilitate the continuation of negative thought patterns even in the face of strong evidence to the contrary.

5. Jumping to Conclusions – Mind Reading This "Jumping to Conclusions" distortion manifests as the inaccurate belief that we know what another person is thinking. Of course, it is possible to have an idea of what other people are thinking, but this distortion refers to the negative interpretations that we jump to.

Seeing a stranger with an unpleasant expression and jumping to the conclusion that they are thinking something negative about you is an example of this distortion.

6. Fortune Telling – Fortune Telling A sister distortion to mind reading, fortune telling refers to the tendency to make conclusions and predictions based on little to no evidence and holding them as gospel truth.

One example of fortune-telling is a young, single woman predicting that she will never find love or have a committed and happy relationship based only on the fact that she has not found it yet. There is simply no way for her to know how her life will turn out, but she sees this prediction as fact rather than one of several possible outcomes.

7. Magnification (Catastrophizing) or Minimization
Also known as the "Binocular Trick" for its stealthy skewing of your perspective, this distortion involves exaggerating or minimizing the meaning, importance, or likelihood of things.

An athlete who is generally a good player but makes a mistake may magnify the importance of that mistake and believe that he is a terrible teammate, while an athlete who wins a coveted award in her sport may minimize the importance of the award and continue believing that she is only a mediocre player.

8. Emotional Reasoning

This may be one of the most surprising distortions to many readers, and it is also one of the most important to identify and address. The logic behind this distortion is not surprising to most people; rather, it is the realization that virtually all of us have bought into this distortion at one time or another.

Emotional reasoning refers to the acceptance of one's emotions as fact. It can be described as "I feel it, therefore it must be true." Just because we feel something doesn't mean it is true; for example, we may become jealous and think our partner has feelings for someone else, but that doesn't make it true. Of course, we know it isn't reasonable to take our feelings as fact, but it is a common distortion, nonetheless.

9. Should Statements

Another particularly damaging distortion is the tendency to make "should" statements. "Should" statements are statements that you make to yourself about what you "should" do, what you "ought" to do, or what you "must" do. They can also be applied to others, imposing a set of expectations that will likely not be met.

When we hang on too tightly to our "should" statements about ourselves, the result is often guilt that we cannot live up to them. When we cling to our "should" statements about others, we are generally disappointed by their failure to meet our expectations, leading to anger and resentment.

10. Labeling and Mislabeling

These tendencies are basically extreme forms of overgeneralization, in which we assign judgments of value to ourselves or to others based on one instance or experience.

For example, a student who labels herself as "an

194

utter fool" for failing an assignment is engaging in this distortion, as is the waiter who labels a customer "a grumpy old miser" if he fails to thank the waiter for bringing his food. Mislabeling refers to the application of highly emotional, loaded, and inaccurate or unreasonable language when labeling.

11. Personalization

As the name implies, this distortion involves taking everything personally or assigning blame to yourself without any logical reason to believe you are to blame.

This distortion covers a wide range of situations, from assuming you are the reason a friend did not enjoy the girls 'night out, to the more severe examples of believing that you are the cause for every instance of moodiness or irritation in those around you.

Though we may not match the physical abilities of Olympic athletes, we can, without a doubt, be as strong as them in the mental game.

Practice perfect practice

To practice anything that's important requires discipline and finesse. Practice doesn't make perfect. Perfect practice makes perfect. You have to take your time and try and do it right.

So, if you want to excel in anything it requires a consistent discipline in practicing perfectly and a deft touch adjusting for the changing topography of everyday life. You can't just wing it and expect good results.

Battle your way through the hedgerow

Just after D-Day the allied advance wanted desperately to sweep their way into Germany and end the war. However, they were impeded by the hedgerows just beyond the beaches that slowed their advance to a crawl. They were stuck, at least for the moment.

Many people are stuck in the hedgerows of relationships, careers, friendships, what have you, slogging it out day in and day out barely getting anywhere. The struggle is fine, we can learn much from it, but when no breakout in life persists, we can usually attribute it to four causes. Each cause cascades down to create the other cause and so on. You can see how each one leads to the other.

-<u>Lack of Purpose</u>. We don't have a deeper meaning or a lofty reason for doing what we're doing. This always manifests itself in always making short term decisions that will continue to keep us stuck in the present.

-<u>Lack of Commitment</u>. We don't stick with it when things don't go our way. We easily throw in the towel and quit before momentum can really pick up.

-<u>Lack of Movement</u>. We become overly cautious and fall back on planning and preparing without really going anywhere. How do you steer a ship? Not with the rudder. You steer a ship by getting it going.

-<u>Lack of Direction</u>. You've heard the old cliché; if you aim at nothing, you'll hit it every time. Doing this creates erratic decision making and unsettled resolve toward anything worthwhile.

On the other hand, if you know where you are going, you can take anyone (including yourself) with you.

So. To break free of these causes of hedgerows and into a more purposeful life requires some action:

Action 1. Embrace the fact that we were made for the struggle and that struggle provides the nutrients for wisdom and strength.

Action 2. Move from quiet desperation to quiet resolve. Stubbornly persist in the face of challenges and follow your own battle plan for getting out of the hedgerow. It won't always be pretty, but it will get you there.

Action 3. Get other people in on your plan. Let them know what you have decided to do and have them hold you accountable for doing it. These are outside eyes and are critical to keeping us focused and on track.

Action 4. Start. Act. Do something. If you're a planning a trip, the first thing you determine is where you are going. The second thing you determine is when are you going to leave. In your journey of life ask yourself where you are going and when you are going to leave.

Put a date on it and then do it!

Slow Down

An interesting study by John Darley and C. Batson entitled "The Good Samaritan" involved having seminary students write a speech. One group was assigned the topic of jobs available after graduation. The other group was given the task of giving a speech on the Good Samaritan.

The parable of the Good Samaritan is about several holy men coming across a wounded person on the road and passing him by. A Samaritan comes across the man and does stop to help.

The students were to deliver the speech in an auditorium on the other side of the campus. They were then given three levels of urgency in giving their speech:

-<u>Low Hurry</u>: "It'll be a few minutes before they're ready for you, but you might as well head on over. If you have to wait over there, it shouldn't be long"

-Intermediate Hurry: "The assistant is ready for you, so please go right over."

-High Hurry: "Oh, you're late. They were expecting you a few minutes ago. You'd better get moving. The assistant should be waiting for you so you'd better hurry. It should take only a minute."

The students passed a person who was part of the experiment. He was groaning, coughing, and huddled in a distressed position. The experimenters wanted to know if they would stop to help this person on their way to their speech and whether that action was based on the topic or the urgency.

The results were as followed:

-Low Hurry: 63 percent

-Intermediate Hurry: 45 percent

-High Hurry: 10 percent.

The topic had nothing to do with the caring response as much as the hurry they were in. Working at a high speed, under stress to get things done quickly, will ultimately reduce the amount of care you exhibit to those closest to you.

Not taking time to slow down will diminish your ability to care for those around you. We need to slow the hell down. I think this pandemic and the awareness of our mortality will do that for us.

Stop ruminating

I had an intuitive sense from the beginning that the movie "John Carter" was going to be a flop. Costing $350 million to make it only brought in $30 million on its opening weekend. Andrew Stanton the director is best known for the direction of "Finding Nemo" and "Wall-E", both wildly successful. He also was a writer for all three "Toy Story" movies.

He is successful, has a track record for creating hit movies and was given a shot to direct his first live action movie. It didn't turn out good. That would be very hard. I have no doubt he is really, really bummed and is questioning his ability to make movies beyond pixelated cartoons.

Though not on that scale, I have had many endeavors that haven't taken off as expected. Huge bummers. I have miffed moments in relationships. No one ever wakes up in the morning intending to tank their day, but the irony is, it's easy to do- by Rumination.

Rumination is the mental choice to dwell on our poor showing whether it is in a relationship or a project. Rumination traps us in the confines of our thoughts about the situation. We begin to create scenarios and reasons that aren't true.

Rumination, in other words, is our way of deceiving ourselves and tanking our efforts to move ahead in a healthy manner. Through our mental lingering we are unable to let go of our mistakes and weak showings.

I'm a master at the art of rumination. It can often trigger my depressive episodes. Here are my suggestions for moving beyond dwelling on bad events and keeping us from tanking ourselves and our day:

-<u>Contemplate</u>. The opposite of rumination is

contemplation. It is the sustained practice of honing the skills of attention to get to the deeper truths of ourselves and our lives.

Contemplation keeps us from applying knee jerk reactions. Take 20 minutes and try to let every thought that enters your mind vanish.

-<u>Move on</u>. Take your perceived errors and move on. Interrogate your thoughts and see them for what they are- perceptions of response. Your perception creates your reality and staying put in them can easily lead to a negative one.

-<u>Do what needs to be done</u>. Ask for forgiveness if needed and take a failure and propel it to maturity.

-<u>Be teachable</u>. Learn from what happened and do better next time. Every day is brand new and offers a chance at a new start.

-<u>Tell yourself the truth</u>. The space between the event and our response is cognitive. We can lie to ourselves about what happened (remember the cognitive distortions) or we can tell ourselves the truth that it isn't as bad as we are prone to think.

So, don't ruminate on things today. It's a sure-fire way to screw it up.

Live with hope

We can live 3 weeks without food; 3 days without water; but only 3 seconds without hope. Even though we aren't guaranteed tomorrow, we still set are alarm to get up in the morning. That is hope.

"For every small box, a lid waits to be removed

For every confining room, a door leads to freedom
For every dark night, a day of brightness will come
For every complex problem, an answer can be found with effort
For every horrible nightmare, an end is certain
For every type of puzzle, a solution lives and waits for discovery"
Bryant L. Court

Don't sabotage your ability to thrive

Sometimes we can be our own worst enemy. It's not that we can't be successful and find fulfillment in life. It's that we too easily sabotage our attempts to do so.

Here are eighteen behaviors, adapted from an amazing list by Dr. Mark Goulston, that can get the better of us and prevent us from thriving.

-Procrastinating. If you're always late on completing tasks, people will stop relying on you and begin resenting you.

-Getting involved with the wrong people. If you continuously get involved with bad people, you'll be the one who has to clean up the mess.

-Saying "yes" when you want to say "no." This results in burnout, loss of credibility and loss of respect from others and yourself.

-Assuming others don't want anything in return. It is human nature to almost always want something in return, even when people say they don't. Thinking ahead about what others might want can save you problems in the future when they try to collect.

-<u>Playing it safe</u>. The world is in a rapid state of change. Doing the same old thing over and over and expecting it to be good enough may turn out to be not so safe.

Always having to be right. This can create resentment and helps build a constituency of people who can't wait to see you fail.

-<u>Focusing on what others are doing wrong.</u> This is a demotivating habit.

-<u>Not learning from your mistakes</u>. Successful people don't make fewer mistakes than unsuccessful people, they just repeat fewer mistakes.

-<u>Talking when nobody's listening</u>. This leads you to think that what you've said is going to be done, when in fact it's not. You will have to repeat the entire process at a later date.

-<u>Taking things too personally.</u> When people take criticism too personally instead of seeing that it is about fixing a problem, the problem becomes larger and takes longer to fix.

-Having unrealistic expectations. When you confuse what is reasonable with what is realistic you set yourself up to fail.

-Trying to take care of everybody. In attempting to take care of everyone, no one
— including you — will be satisfied.

-Refusing to "play games." Politics, schmoozing and small talk are all necessary in order to succeed. Putting them down because you do them poorly is costly.

-Being envious of others. Teamwork is ruined when team members envy each other to the extent that they root against each other.

-Quitting too soon. If you always quit, you'll never succeed; if you always try, you'll eventually succeed.

-Letting fear run your life. If you let fear run your life, it might just run you out of your job.
-Not moving on after a loss. When you spend

more time mourning your losses than you do moving ahead, you can't move ahead.

-<u>Not asking for what you need</u>. If you don't ask for what you need — whether it be for someone to help you do your job or for a promotion — you're leaving it to other people's imaginations.

Use everything you got

I read Steve Martin's autobiography of his stand up days. Titled *Born Standing Up,* it recounted the manic delivery of his comedy and his rapidly rising popularity in the early days of his career. He immersed himself in divergent interests. He was into magic and worked at the shop at Disneyland. He made balloon animals. He played the banjo.

He questioned the value of spending precious time on all those things. After all, how lucrative is blowing up and bending balloons and playing the banjo with a toy arrow stuck through his head?

Then he wrote about his first appearance on the Tonight Show with Johnny Carson.

He did his whole manic, balloon, banjo, arrow thing. When he was finished, Johnny asked him to sit next to him during the commercial break. That is a huge honor and was hardly afforded comedians. After Steve sat down Johnny leaned over and whispered in his ear, "You'll use everything".

Everything suddenly clicked for Steve Martin. All those seemingly wasted hours in seemingly trivial pursuits were all being used for his success. Nothing was wasted.

Think back on all your pursuits and interests. Some might seem unrelated. Heck, you might not even be in a profession that aligns with the degree you spent a lot of money on getting in college. Rest assured, everything you've learned and tried over the years (even the less than noble pursuits) are all being put to good use. Even any of my pursuits fueled by mania. You are the totality of your actions and interests, and you will, if you aren't already, use everything...

Don't almost do anything

In this global coronavirus pandemic, it's easy to wallow, to let fear paralyze us from doing what we ᵢeed to do. According to research by survival psychologist John Leach, when a random group of people finds itself in a sudden emergency like a fire or a natural disaster, 10 to 15 percent will consistently freak out, 10 to 20 percent will stay cool, and the rest will become dazed and hesitant sheep.

The twenty percent that stays cool, engaging tough situations with calm and confidence, are decisive people. They make decisions and go after them. They don't hesitate. They don't almost do something. They know that speed of execution is key to success and essential for resilience. Even a bad decision is better than no decision at all.

Life is ambiguous. If we wait for absolute certainty before deciding, then we may never act. You can't wait to take a trip until all the lights are green.
You'll never go. Trying to always make the 'right' decision assumes that life is always simple or even simplistic. Yeah, right.

Sometimes there are no 'right 'decisions, only alternative ones. The point is to keep acting on them and learning along the way. To do something.

Imagine there are five frogs on a log. One of the frog
decides to jump. How many frogs are left on the log?
Still five- there is a big difference between deciding to
jump and actually jumping. All decisions that are acted
on strengthen the muscle of resilience and resolve.

As Conrad Hilton pointed out, "Success…is connected
with action. Successful people keep moving. They
make mistakes, but they don't quit." They decide not
to…

Make the Hard Choice

Every day you're confronted with a choice. In the
stress and strain of everyday life, you have to choose
between two different mindsets. I believe doing this is
the hardest thing you'll do each day.
The choice is between allowing either a weakened
mindset or a resilient mindset to direct your day. That
choice determines how your day is structured and your
effectiveness in engaging its stress.

A weakened mindset tells you you're ill equipped to
handle challenges and so you respond with a weakened
resolve. A weakened mindset creates inadequate
thoughts that are easy to adopt. They're the "I can't…"

or "I should…" statements. They don't require anything from you but to give in. In fact, they can become excuses for not doing anything.

A resilient mindset, on the other hand, is hard to implement. It takes an act of the will. It requires a constant vigilance against weakened, ineffectual thoughts. You won't always want to deal with difficult situations, but you WILL because that is what resilience requires. It takes discipline and daily practice. You can choose resilience in the following ways:

> -<u>Begin each day with the conscious resolve to confront stinky thinking</u>. The first thought when you get up each morning should be one of strength to tackle the day. Tell yourself you can and you will engage the challenges with a gritty resolve. This daily conditioning will create a habit of thought that will carry over to the rest of the day.
>
> -<u>Interrogate your thoughts and determine their effectiveness.</u> Ask yourself if the thoughts are diminishing your ability to resist stress. Remember vulnerable thoughts are the white

flags of surrender. Don't give in or take the easy way out.

-Counteract a deceiving mindset with the truth. Are you really that incapable of going where you need to go or doing what you need to do? Of course not. People who survived the holocaust did so because they knew their captors could never take away the efficacy of their inner experience.

-Interface with others that care for you. A resilient mindset is not embarrassed or too proud to ask for help. Give people the privilege of ministering to you in tough times. Spending time in relationships helps sharpen your resolve. It also normalizes any challenges you experience- you're not alone.

It takes tough, concerted effort, but anything worthwhile does. The difficulty in choosing a resilient mindset is why so many people spend their days vulnerable to anxiety instead.

Create Magic

When you experience chaotic change, you find yourself smack in the middle of disorientation. It is a place of potentialities- it can be an opportunity for honest self-assessment or damaging self-deception. The tipping point is in the ancient art of magic, the oldest impulse of the human soul. Perhaps because it is the deepest. The following thoughts are from the rich insights of Ruben A. Alves.

Why do humans create magic? When the natives of Trobriand Islands were to fish in the inner lagoon there were no magical ceremonies for the occasion. The situation changed however, when they had to go out to sea. Now the whole process was carefully prepared by magic. Why? The reason was simple. In the lagoon they had a sense of self-assurance and control. There was no danger. Their lives were not being risked.

The deep sea, however, took their self-confidence away. The game was dangerous. They were gambling their lives. In one situation they had a sense of power, in the other a feeling of impotence.

Man practices magic when he feels he lacks power to

carry out his intention by means of his own resources. That is, when encountering chaotic change there is an obstacle that brings our activity to a halt. Our intention is frustrated. We experience reality as it is. We are absent our omnipotence. That is a good thing and opens us up to the magical, to the mystical, to God.

Be fully alive

In other words, be vibrantly mortal.
An Army veteran named John Crabtree had been receiving benefits from the government. Evidently, he had been wounded in Vietnam and was now on permanent disability. One day, out of the blue, he received an official notification from the government of his own death. Needless to say, this was quite a shock!

Mr. Crabtree wrote the government a letter stating that he was indeed very much alive and would like to continue receiving his benefits. The letter did no good. He then tried calling the government. (This was a very time-consuming process). The phone calls didn't change the situation either. Finally, as a last resort, the veteran contacted a local television station, which ran a human-interest story about his situation.

During the interview, the reporter asked him, "How do you feel about this whole ordeal?" The veteran chuckled and said, "Well, I feel a little frustrated by it. After all, have you ever tried to prove that you're alive?"

That's a pretty good question for all of us. Could you prove that you are alive? Really, genuinely, deep-down alive? When was the last time you had an alive moment? Not the last time you took a breath or had your heart beat inside your chest, but the last time you felt yourself alive to your living, alive to your loving, deeply present with the gift of life itself?

Seize the Day and be committed to making every second count!!

Be Resilient

Mortality can show how resilient the human spirit is. When rubber hits the road, we have the capacity to valiantly rise to any occasion. We have an uncanny knack to figure things out. From becoming a new parent to transitioning to college far away from home, to living through a pandemic, we learn to thrive no matter what. So, don't ever think you don't have what it takes to flourish. It's written in your DNA.

Resilient people are characterized by actions, events and experiences which collectively embody the qualities that enable one not only to overcome what others may experience as disasters, but to utilize such experiences to bounce back to an exhilarating resolve. We can't stop change but we can choose how we respond to it.

The really good news is that resilience is not an inborn personality trait, but a set of skills and attitudes that can be learned, dynamics that provoke our ability to bounce and thrive.

Here are some of the dynamics of resilience:

> -Resilience is knowing the nature and ramifications of the changes we experience

> -Resilience is engaging the ramifications of change with courage and honesty

> -Resilience is navigating life with an unwavering resolve to succeed

-Resilience is perceiving success as living out the core reason for who they are

-Resilience is embracing uncertainty and finding unexpected, untapped opportunities

-Resilience is relating richly with others for support in tough situations.

-Resilience is allowing mistakes to provide the fuel for innovation

-Resilience is living effectively in the moment; and leveraging opportunities.

Never underestimate the power of Selfless Acts

During World War II, a Jewish woman was riding a city bus home from work when SS storm troopers suddenly stopped the coach and began examining the identification papers of passengers. Most were annoyed, but a few were terrified. Jews were being told to leave the bus and get into a truck around the corner.

The woman watched from her seat in the rear as the

soldiers systematically worked their way down the aisle. She began to tremble, tears streaming down her face. When the man next to her noticed that she was crying, he politely asked why.

"I don't have the papers you have. I am a Jew. They're going to take me."

The man exploded in disgust. He began to curse and scream at her. "You stupid bitch," he roared. "I can't stand being near you!"

The SS men asked what all the yelling was about. "Damn her," the man shouted angrily. "My wife has forgotten her papers again! I'm so fed up. She always does this!"

The soldiers laughed and moved on. There are times when a task that only you can do finds you. It is at that moment you have to fulfill part of your destiny, to be who it is you were truly meant to be. Vibrantly Mortal people know that such moments arise at unexpected times and in unfamiliar places.

They are ready and willing enough to respond to moments of self-sacrifice, even risk. They know that all of us are in this thing called life together, and the actions of one can impact the lives of many. It often all funnels down to the power of seemingly trivial acts.

Rely on your tugboats

A British nuclear submarine ran aground on some rocks off the west coast of Scotland. It is one of the most technologically sophisticated vessels on the planet which makes the incident that much more ironic.

What I found interesting, though, was the way they freed the sub so it could continue on in open waters. Officials waited for high tide and then used tugboats to tow her out. Tugboats as you know are the unsung workhorses of the nautical world.

It got me to thinking. Whenever we get stuck or mired down in the muck and the grime of life's circumstances, what are the tugboats we used to tow us out and free us to move on? What are the workhorses that are critical when needed?
The following are my tugboats:

> -Friends who are always available, 24/7, to do the heavy lifting when I can't (and is always

reciprocated when needed).

-<u>Mental tenacity</u>. I admit that this tugboat is one of my most powerful but one I neglect to my peril. It is amazing how much I diminish its ability to pull me out by too easily falling into unhealthy and unhelpful thought patterns. This tugboat is slowly getting stronger.

-<u>Faith</u>. Without a belief in a power and person much more powerful than me, I will continually run aground and stay stuck much, much longer. This tugboat must continually be fine-tuned and maintained through the spiritual disciplines of prayer and solitude.

-<u>Humor</u>. Sometimes the thing I need most to move me on is a healthy and honest laugh at the situation. Laughing is very serious business, and the ability to laugh at ourselves is one of the best ways to admit our foibles and weaknesses.

I'm sure there are more tugboats in my life when I'm stuck, but these are the primary one's in my fleet. I may think I got it all together and that I have all the bells and whistles of a sophisticated nuclear sub, but no technique or technology can free me quite like the tugboats.

What are the tugboats in your life, the unsung workhorses that are always available when needed? Always remember them and be grateful for the power they provide to our lives.

Keep Calm and Carry On

During the horrific Battle of Britain when the German Luftwaffe was pounding London with bombs, the threat of invasion was extremely high. The British government produced a series of posters in order to raise morale. One such poster, not widely used, was intended to be posted in the case of an actual invasion by the Nazis. It stated simply to "Keep Calm and Carry On".

During the invasion of this pandemic in our lives, the sentiment to "Keep Calm and Carry On" couldn't be more relevant:

> -Keeping Calm means having the stubborn resolve to stay mentally steady in upheavals. It's

tough. Some of us are over reactors to events. Some are ambivalent about them, and some are just downright despairing. Hope jolts us into another way of perceiving. In the midst of the Battle of Britain, Winston Churchill kept a steady resolve to never give in and encourage the British people with hope to never surrender. He kept them calm. As a result, Britain was never invaded and the beginning of the end of the war was realized.

Keeping calm requires a stubborn hope that inspires a committed resolve – a resolve to carry on.

-Carrying On means answering the big "Why?". That is, what is the purpose for which you live? This goes beyond just making money (which can vanish quickly) or saving for retirement (which isn't guaranteed). What is your life for, really? What is its purpose, really?

To answer those questions first begins with hope – hope for a future that keeps us calm enough to reflect on the answers. The big "Why?" for

Winston Churchill and the British people was to overcome the tyranny of Nazism. After all, life must have deeper meaning than just recessionary panics and momentary despair. Once you've determined your big "Why?", nothing can keep you from carrying on.

Hope. Just Hope

Things have been a bummer lately. The economy is tight, and the pandemic is in full force. How does one persist in hope when things seem so hopeless? Here are my suggestions based on the acronym H.O.P.E.

> **H:** Hone your mental fortitude. This is a way of thinking that lead us to respond in patterned ways to the everyday demands of life. Research shows that how or what we think directly affects our moods and how we feel. Events or circumstances do not determine your mood. How you think about them does. Keep your thoughts in check. Remember, you are responsible for your own emotions and actions. Your harmful actions or dysfunctional behavior are the product of your irrational thinking. Take responsibility for your distress.

O: Optimize your moments. Life is a daisy chain of moments all weaving together the tapestry we call life. Each moment is laden with potential. It is the only part of time in which we can be fully aware. Celebrate the glass of wine with your spouse. Laugh heartily at stupid jokes. Weep at the injustices of life. In other words, deeply seize the day by the moments.

P: Populate your relationships. None of us is as smart as all of us. Getting through bummer times cannot be done alone. You need others to share the load and contribute insights. Given the nature of social media we can find others who care over long distances. Of course, it is critical to have a handful of friends who are close by to lend a hand to and shoulder to cry on. Plus, as you contribute to the relationship you get a greater sense of self-worth.

E: Energize your soul. You cannot neglect your spiritual nature. St. Augustine said of our relationship with God, "our hearts are restless until we find our rest in you". Settle down and breath in the reality of a greater, more expansive world. Rest in the relationship of a God who cares and can be trusted. You might not always understand what he is up to, but you can be faithful to him as he is to you through thick or thin.

CONCLUSION: WHERE ARE WE AT IN HUMAN HISTORY?

It's important to recognize where we are. This is brand new stretch of water. It's Crunch Time, a disorienting moment of change rife with such extraordinary potentiality that people are faced with the transformative decision on how to get through it. Professor Walter Brueggemann writes that there are three major stages of orientation that reflect even the seasons of our own lives.

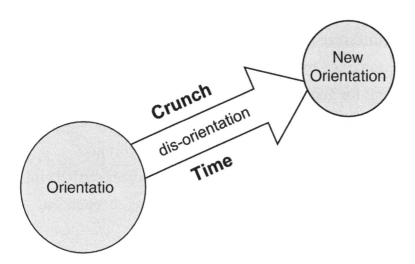

The first stage is being "securely oriented". It is here that we feel settled and secure. Our lives make sense and the decisions we make are anchored in good judgement. This could be a time when your job seems secure and your family life is well ordered. Financially we are doing okay. Yet we know that this security never hangs around for long. Which leads us to the second stage.

The second stage is being "painfully disoriented". These are times when we feel blindsided, hurt, and reeling from stress and the perceived enormity of change. Here you may have lost a job, a child, a divorce or some other chaotic and unexpected event. Yet if we persist in this movement, hang on with resilience, the third stage inevitable reveals itself.

This third stage is "surprisingly newly orientated". This stage is marked by surprise, the way things all seemed to work out for good and gives us something new out of something old. When we are in this stage, life seems renewed and our circumstances are compellingly welcomed. Over time this new place becomes settled and secure and we begin the process of moving through the stages all over again.

Right now, we are in a stage of painful disorientation. I call it CRUNCH TIME. We suddenly find ourselves in a tough life and death environment. We have drifted out of the current of a known world and into the vortex of a completely strange, new world. It's in-between what was and what will be. It will be surprising to see where this all leads us.

...And So, During this time of the Covid-19 virus and the subsequent full on awareness of our mortality...

There is a story of a man who had a recurrent dream that he was being pursued by a ferocious, terrifying lion. The fear and subsequent retreat for his life left him exhausted and weakened. He would eventually wake himself up with terrifying screams.

As he recounted the dream to a friend, his friend suggested that next time in the dream he should confront the lion head on and figure out who or what he was doing in the man's life.

A few nights later he had the dream of the lion chasing him. Instead of running away, the man turned and engaged the lion with terrifying roars and teeth meant to shred through flesh. In fear, the man asked, "Who are you? What do you want?" The lion replied, "I am your courage and your strength! Why do you keep running away from me?"

That is a great little story. The fear of fear is worse than the fear itself. Flip the perspective of your death in your life. See it as an opportunity to find the courage you need. You can't run away from it, no one can. Life is filled with adversity, setbacks, losses, and death. So, turn and face it and find the courage you need to overcome.

This potent awareness of your mortality that you currently face has all the inherent resources you need to thrive. Sometimes you don't need to look any further for help than within the crisis itself. Sounds impossible?

Just consider that inherent within every crisis is its openness to be shaped. How? Through the power of your perception. This is your explanatory style (see cognitive distortions). You can explain tough and stressful events either through positive or negative explanations. The crisis will conform to the perception. What is your default thought process when confronted with a challenge? Is it shaping the crisis with engaging or retreating perceptions?

Inherent within crisis is its humility to allow others to act. When I was going through a very tough bout of depression my counselor told me I needed to give people the honor of ministering to me. That was tough. I always wanted to be the one who was counted on to help.

It was humbling to think I needed help from others. But the crisis allowed me to give to others the honor of helping. You know what? All were available and willing to be there for me when I needed it.

Crisis provides the gift of wisdom. Remember what I mentioned about "scar tissue"? It is the wounds that crisis inflicts that give us the depth of insight and wisdom toward life we couldn't get without our awareness of death giving it them to us…

So, this time of coronavirus and subsequent awareness of our mortality will produce, I believe, a generation of people that will be vibrantly mortal like we've never seen before. Look out world!

A Couple of Interesting Resources

There is an online questionnaire that contains a number of statements related to different attitudes toward death. You can gauge your attitude toward death by working your way through the statements. Fascinating.

- http://www.drpaulwong.com/documents/wong-scales/death-attitude-profile-revised-scale.pdf

In the tiny Himalayan country of Bhutan, they believe engaging death five times a day is the way to a better life. In fact, it has been recognized as the happiest country on earth. Along that philosophy, an app was created that sends you quotes 5 times a day to remind you of your mortality. It is one of the best apps I have.

- https://www.wecroak.com

Caitlin Doughty is a mortician, activist, and funeral industry rabble-rouser. In 2011 she founded the death acceptance collective The Order of the Good Death, which has spawned the death positive movement.

- http://caitlindoughty.com

For more on a Whole Assin' philosophy and approach to life visit: https://www.wholeassinit.com

Made in the USA
Monee, IL
22 September 2023

43171515R00142